Education and the Environment

SUNY Series, Global Conflict and Peace Education

Betty A. Reardon, Editor

SUNY Series, Environmental Public Policy

Lester W. Milbrath, Editor

Education and the Environment

Learning to Live with Limits

Gregory A. Smith

State University of New York Press

Published by
State University of New York Press, Albany

For information, address State University of New York
Press, State University Plaza, Albany, N.Y., 12246

Production by M. R. Mulholland
Marketing by Fran Keneston

Library of Congress Cataloging-in-Publication Data

Smith, Gregory A., 1948–
      Education and the environment : learning to live with limits /
   Gregory A. Smith.
            p.   cm. — (SUNY series, global conflict and peace education)
   (SUNY series, environmental public policy)
      Includes bibliographical references and index.
      ISBN 0–7914–1137–0. — ISBN 0–7914–1138–9 (pbk.)
      1. Education—Social aspects—United States. 2. Education—
   Environmental aspects—United States. 3. Education—Economic
   aspects—United States. 4. Educational change—United States.
   I. Title. II. Series. III. Series: SUNY series, environmental
   public policy.
   LC191.4.S64.   1992
   370.19'0973—dc20

                                                                      91–30788
                                                                      CIP

10 9 8 7 6 5 4 3 2

For Ethan, Paul, and Eliot

Contents

Acknowledgments

The years I spent composing and revising this book were graced with important moments during which the mutual support and interdependence that became such compelling issues for me in the text were realized in my dealings with others. In this sense, the work that follows is really a collective product, for without the care, support, encouragement, and guidance of teachers, friends, and family, I might have abandoned this project long ago.

Mary Metz and Daniel Pekarsky, professors in the Department of Educational Policy Studies at the University of Wisconsin-Madison, prodded and sustained me throughout this process. They consistently demonstrated faith in my ability to accomplish the task I set for myself. My work with Michael Apple was also pivotal to the development of the conceptual framework that undergirds my thought. Classes and discussions with him helped me begin to understand the way contradictions inherent in our way of life may in time necessitate some of the cultural transformations I outline here. Although he was not immediately involved with the writing of this book, Gary Wehlage initiated me into the realm of educational research and policymaking through direct experience. Thanks to my work with him, I began to grasp the degree to which alternative programs for at-risk students could provide an entry-point for more substantial systemic changes of American schools.

A number of friends have also played an important role in seeing this project through. Henry St. Maurice was an ongoing source of ideas and additional resources. Jim Lorman offered an important sounding-board for my uncertainties and confusion. Our regular discussions about the environmental crisis and the construction of alternative social realities laid the foundation for the final form that this book has taken. Parker Palmer helped me think through ideas about community and individualism and the role of education as a vehicle for change. Robert Aitken offered steady guidance and a model of spiritual and social engagement. Michael Jones was a faithful reader of my efforts and provided useful criticism regarding the text. Years ago, Bob Heyerman helped me to define some of the commitments that have evolved into my current work.

More recently, Priscilla Ross at SUNY Press has provided invaluable assistance in helping me turn a dissertation into a book. I've greatly valued her interest in and commitment to this project. Mary Clark's enthusiasm also has been a source of reassurance.

Finally, my family provided ongoing support and needed distraction. My wife, Rebecca, has given me unremitting encouragement and the time required for research and writing. My young sons, Ethan, Paul, and Eliot, reminded me of the delight in living that in the end should inform all our efforts. This book is for them.

One

❁

Changing Conditions— Changing Schools

In the 1980s and early 1990s, education has once more come to the center of public debate. Issues related to cultural diversity, school governance, parental choice, school dropouts, and the declining achievement of American students have become the stuff of countless news articles and television broadcasts. One of the primary characteristics of this debate has been its focus on the link between education and economic productivity and the need to upgrade the performance of American students if we, as a nation, are to continue competing successfully in an increasingly global market. A central preoccupation of recent educational discourse has been the way in which the transition to a postindustrial, nonmanufacturing economy has necessitated major changes in the kind of education Americans offer their young.

This debate points to the close connection between economic practices and other cultural institutions. It is therefore not surprising that among those who have been most vocal in their calls for dramatic educational reform are the representatives of America's corporate sector, one of whom is now Deputy Secretary of Education. Focused as this debate has been on the immediate threat to America's well-being posed by more competitive industrial nations, discussions regarding U.S. schools have ignored entirely what may in fact be a much more serious long-term threat to our economy and common welfare: the environmental crisis and the depletion of the energy sources upon which our entire social structure depends. Although the environmental crisis has not yet begun to make itself felt in obvious ways, it has become an increasingly insistent theme in our daily lives. Consumed as we are with the tasks of the moment, however, few of us have begun to consider the implications of these crises for common institutions like the schools.

This book is an effort to interject environmental considerations into the current discourse about U.S. education. It is predicated on the assumption that a continued expansion of the forces of production may well be impeded by ecological factors beyond human control, and that this closing of the era of material progress will have a profound impact on the configuration of our social relations. This impact may be as significant as that which accompanied the process of modernization, itself. Among the changes that are likely to be generated by an environmentally necessitated decline in material production will be a transformation of the relationship between the individual and the broader society. In the long period of economic expansion that has been the hallmark of the modern era, it has been possible for individuals to achieve a level of independence from kin group and the larger community unheard of in agricultural or hunting and gathering societies. Given the prospect of apparently limitless economic growth, the twentieth century has seen a sizeable proportion of citizens in developed nations acquire the ability to create for themselves and their offspring the personal security that has been one of the central goals of the middle class. This desire for security, though individualistic, has not necessarily been egotistically selfish; it has, however, been anticollectivist, contributing to a growing atomization of American society and a withdrawal from public life of increasing numbers of citizens.

One of the primary vehicles for the creation of individual security has been public education and the access it has provided to the occupational opportunities that have accompanied an expanding economy. Through schooling children ideally acquire both the skills and the social norms required to negotiate the economic and political institutions that dominate contemporary society. These norms have often functioned in ways that diminish children's ties to their homes and communities, freeing them to participate in a dynamic and ever-changing market society. Although the alienating consequences of this form of socialization have been tolerable during the preceding era of economic growth, current ecological developments may jeopardize the ability of increasing numbers of people to create acceptable levels of personal security for themselves outside the context of mutually supportive human associations.

The environmental, political, social, and economic crises we are beginning to encounter now and are likely to encounter in coming decades lie outside the control of individuals. Addressing or reversing them will almost certainly require collective action both at local and international levels. We may possess, however, neither the orientation nor the skills to enter effectively into such collective action. The socialization most of us have encountered in middle-class homes and in most American schools has been primarily pointed in the opposite direction—toward independence, self-reliance, and the shaking off of impediments to personal freedom. To learn to deal with the new material reality coming into shape around us may require the mastering of other social relations, ones more appropriate for an era of restricted, rather than seemingly unlimited, opportunities. Given the reduced strength of the home, the neighborhood, and churches, schools may provide one of the few sites where children could learn the social relations and skills they will need to grapple with these fundamental changes in the material basis of our common existence.

As they are presently shaped, schools are poorly suited for this task. By preparing children to think of themselves as individuals who must sell their talents in a competitive job market if they are to succeed, schools erode social collectivities more than they support them. To respond to the changing environmental conditions we are likely to encounter in the coming decades, educators will need to develop an educational process that cultivates a very different set of expectations and norms. If they do not, our children could well lack the social skills and dispositions needed to foster their own survival.

These skills and dispositions must include the ability to cooperate and enter into alliances with others to solve common problems and to recognize the fundamental interdependence that people share with one another. Only as children come to see that their well-being depends on the well-being of others will they begin to reclaim and reshape the patterns of mutual support that have sustained human communities throughout millenia. Schools, as well, must acquaint their students with a very different approach to the natural world, one that acknowledges its finitude and the need to weigh the consequences of human activity against the welfare of the environment as a whole. No longer can we afford to believe that the pursuit of self-interest, or even the apparent interest of human society, inevitably contributes to the common good. That "good" must be served with a consciousness of social and environmental costs, and with accompanying self-restraint. Socializing students to this new reality will require making significant modifications in the nature of American education as it currently exists.

Unraveling the Modern World

Before embarking on a consideration of what these educational changes may be, it is important to explore in more detail why a transformation in environmental conditions will interfere with the ability of American citizens to create the personal security and freedom from communal ties that has been one of the central aims of our way of life from the early 1800s on. Biologists and ecologists have described a sequence of events that other species encounter if they mistreat the environment. The first of these states is known as *draw-down*. During this period, the perpetuation of the species can lead its members to undercut the ability of necessary resources to replenish themselves. Unless this situation is reversed—for example, through migration—this process will continue until a threshold known as *overshoot* is passed. Overshoot occurs when "the use of resources in an ecosystem exceeds its carrying capacity and there is no way to recover or replace what was lost" (Sale, 1985, 24). Once past the threshold of overshoot, the species experiences mass starvation that reduces its population to a level supportable by the ecosystem. If the ecosystem has been too severely damaged, however, such a crash can lead to a total species *die-out*.

Kirkpatrick Sale compares our present situation to that of yeast in a wine vat (1985, 26). Human beings have thrived beyond measure as a result of our own inventiveness and the discovery of sources of energy that at least temporarily gave us the power to reshape the natural environment to suit our own purposes. Coal, oil, and natural gas have been the sugar upon which we have supported this growth, but like the sweet, rotting grapes in a wine vat, they are quickly being turned into poisons that are destroying the environment's ability to support our lives. Although we continue to hope that some new source of energy—more abundant and less polluting than fossil fuels—will be found to replace those that have undergirded the industrial revolution, such hope forestalls the necessity of recognizing the limitations imposed by the finite and malleable content of the wine vat itself. There is a strong possibility that, like yeast, we will be unable to stop before we have irremediably polluted the source of our own nourishment. If we continue acting as though there are no limits to the possibilities opened by our inventiveness and power, this will be the likely result.

Lester Brown and Sandra Postel (1987) of the Worldwatch Institute point out that we are not the first civilization to face the possibility of a major deterioration of environmental support systems and the dangers engendered by such a collapse. Four thousand years ago in

Mesopotamia, large-scale irrigation projects dramatically increased agricultural productivity. Though these projects supported the growth of the first civilizations encountered in the archaeological record, the absence of underground drainage for irrigated land eventually led to the salinization of some of the most fertile soil in the ancient world. Over several hundred years, crop yields dropped by 65 percent or more, eventually contributing to the decline and then devolution of the first human experiments in large-scale social organization.

The classic Mayan civilization experienced a similar decline after 750 A.D. At one point, this society supported a population of five million. Within less than two centuries, this number dropped to one-tenth its previous level. Although scholars are uncertain about the precise reasons for this collapse, many believe that the overburdening of a limited ecosystem by a growing population was a central contributing factor. Brown and Postel (1987) cite a mathematical model developed by anthropologist John W. G. Lowe that describes the way in which different stress factors, including food shortage, could have triggered the disintegration of this once flourishing society. His model parallels the phases of draw-down, overshoot, and collapse discussed by Sale.

The experiences of the Mesopotamians and the Mayans can serve as object lessons about the vulnerability of humankind and our dependence upon the natural world. What distinguishes modern/industrial civilization from these earlier societies, however, is the extent to which human activities have become global rather than merely regional. Whereas the activities of the civilizations described damaged the carrying capacity of circumscribed ecosystems, our activities threaten the biosphere as a whole.

In the early 1970s and then in an updated version in 1980, Robert Heilbroner surveyed current studies regarding the environmental consequences of industrialism and presented his *Inquiry Into the Human Prospect*. His analysis is not unlike that of Kirkpatrick Sale. He identifies the problem as growth—both in terms of numbers and in terms of our increasing ability to exploit the biosphere for our own purposes. Heilbroner argues that behind this growth is our preoccupation with the continued expansion of the forces of production, a preoccupation that has been central to the success of capitalism; if this expansion is not checked, however, we face the almost certain prospect of the malfunctioning of natural systems.

In place of capitalism and the acquisitive culture that sustains it, Heilbroner suggests that we must create a way of life in which frugality, simplicity, and the pursuit of nonmaterial ends are primary values. In doing so, we may be able to protect needed resources for future generations and prevent the disasters that will await us if we refuse to contain our desire for increasing levels of material comfort. Although such sacrifices may be painful, Heilbroner asserts that they are imperative if we are concerned about more than the limited sphere of our own temporal existence.[1] Although one may disagree with Heilbroner's assertion that our only salvation may lie in the creation of a highly authoritarian State, it is hard to argue with his portrait of the planet's limits and their implications for continued industrial growth, as well as the burgeoning of our own numbers.

Even taking just one set of resources, fossil fuels, it becomes clear that our way of life can be supported for little more than another century. Data from the *International Energy Annual* (1988), published by the U.S. Department of Energy, suggest that we are living on borrowed time. In 1988, for example, world oil consumption was 23.4 billion barrels. Known reserves equal 990.6 billion barrels. If there were no increase in usage rates and no increase in available reserves, this would leave us with 42 years of oil. Currently, estimated undiscovered recoverable oil resources increase potential reserves only to 1060 to 1720 billion barrels, giving us at most 75 more years.

Although conservation and the discovery of additional oil reserves could extend this period to some extent, a more important yet generally ignored aspect of this issue is the question of oil production. As oil companies are forced to exploit reserves located in geographical regions not amenable to drilling (e.g., the Arctic or deep water locations in the Gulf of Mexico), costs of extraction and transport will rise. As Riva (1983) reports, unless oil prices go up as well, it will not be in the interest of energy corporations to develop these fields.

> Already the capital costs per daily oil production in some areas of the North Sea are forty times the costs in the Middle East. Over 11,000 man-years are required to construct the largest of the North Sea gravity production platforms; the cost would exceed that of a nuclear power plant or oil refinery. The guyed tower constructed for oil production in 1,000 feet of water in the Gulf of Mexico will recover oil at about sixty-five times Middle East production costs. As oil production moves into the frontier basins in deeper waters or under Arctic ice, these costs will further escalate and be reflected in the world economy. (xxi–xxii).

It goes without saying that environmental risks associated with such energy production will increase as well. What this will mean is that although we may continue to draw upon remaining reserves for a number of years, the long period of cheap and easily accessible energy that has sustained industrial development throughout the twentieth century is coming to an end.

The dilemma of rising energy costs will accompany the use of alternatives to oil as well. Although natural gas, nuclear plants, and solar, wind, hydro, and geothermal power could well replace petroleum in the short and perhaps long term, their development is unlikely to be as inexpensive and profitable as oil. Though temporarily abundant, natural gas, like petroleum, is a finite resource. And, though attractive, the development of nonfossil fuel sources of energy will require the investment of vast amounts of capital, which may or may not be available depending upon the point at which industrial societies decide that they must curb their addiction to oil. The fate of the nuclear power industry over the previous decade is indicative of the problem of capitalizing new sources of power. When costs threaten to exceed potential returns, investors become scarce. Furthermore, it is unlikely that public works projects capable of sponsoring the development of alternative energy sources (e.g., the building of hydroelectric dams) will enjoy wide governmental support in a period of increasing fiscal indebtedness. Assuming that alternative energy sources will be capable of sustaining the ever-increasing expansion of the forces of production that underlies our civilization is therefore problematic.

Even if fossil fuel reserves were unlimited, it is unlikely that we would be able to continue utilizing them in the way we are now. As is commonly known, the burning of petroleum and coal appears to be leading to climatic changes that could seriously affect agricultural productivity, as well as the habitability of coastal areas around the planet. This is the reason that, even though vast reserves of coal remain to be exploited, their use could well cause more damage to industrial civilization than support. Midcontinental regions in the Northern Hemisphere responsible for a major share of the world's grain production could well be subject to higher temperatures and lower rainfall if we continue to burn oil and coal as our major sources of energy (Postel, 1987). The consequences would be even greater if we turned to coal as our primary energy source. The drought of 1988, possibly symptomatic of global warming, at minimum demonstrates the consequences of hotter summers and diminished rainfall on crop yields. In this year, U.S. corn production fell by an average of 37 percent, and soybean production by 23 percent (Samuelson, 1988). Although the effect of an occasional bad year can be offset by surpluses from years of higher productivity, a steady series of poor years would have a profound impact on not only the profitability of American agriculture, but the ability of U.S. farmers to feed our own population. Unrestricted industrial growth could therefore eventually affect our capacity to provide basic necessities for coming generations.

Other forms of pollution—of water, of land, of food—all threaten to have a deleterious impact on human health, as well as the health of other species. In our efforts to increase our level of material comfort and security we—like the Mesopotamians and Mayans before us—have eroded the viability of the life systems that support us. As Brown and Postel (1987) note:

> A frustrating paradox is emerging. Efforts to improve living standards are themselves beginning to threaten the health of the global economy. The very notion of progress begs for redefinition in light of the intolerable consequences unfolding as a result of its pursuit.... The scale of human activities has begun to threaten the habitability of the earth itself. (4–5)

At the heart of our current crisis, however, is an even more disarming paradox than the one acknowledged by Brown and Postel. Our way of life depends upon consumption. Without it, the engines of industry and profitability cannot be maintained. When these are slowed, the results are unemployment and social disorder. And yet with consumption come the relentless exhaustion of resources and environmental damage that will eventually render the economic practices of the modern world obsolete. Moving to the world of simple frugality envisioned by Heilbroner and necessitated by a recognition of limits will require us to imagine collective rather than individualistic social structures that will enable all people to meet fundamental needs for food, shelter, and health care. If we do not, individuals will continue to seek the goods they believe are necessary to give them the illusion of security in an unpredictable world (see Wachtel, 1988); the social consequences of this form of competitive accumulation will be devastating.

Throughout the 1980s, workers in the United States received a taste of what can occur when production is reduced outside the context of alternative structures of social support and collective action. Although this decline in productivity was the result of the exportation of many U.S. manufacturing firms to nations where labor is less costly, the consequences of "capital flight" provide a useful object lesson of what is likely to occur when the declining availability of cheap energy or increasingly restrictive pollution standards lead to a reduction in industrial output.

Since the mid-1970s, millions of formerly well-paid workers have been laid off. Between 1980 and 1987 alone, two to three million high-value jobs were eliminated as a result of foreign competition. Another nine million high-value jobs were lost as a result of automation, mergers, plant closings, and overhead reduction measures (Noble, 1986; Seabury, 1987a). Although many of these jobs have been replaced, new positions are generally in low-paid occupations such as janitors, nurses' aides, salesclerks, cashiers, and waiters and waitresses (Reich 1983). After a review of U.S. Labor Department projections, Levin and Rumberger (1983) concluded that

> As a whole, employment growth in the United States will favor the low- and middle-level occupations.... By 1990, jobs in all professional and managerial occupations will account for only 28 percent of all employment growth, less than in either of the previous two decades. In contrast, clerical and service occupations will account for 40 percent of total employment growth in the 1980s. (19)

Current projections from 1986 to 2000 reveal the same pattern (Department of Commerce, 1988, 375). The result of these trends has been a steadily falling median household income (Seabury, 1987b) and the growing impoverishment of a significant proportion of the American population.

What has been particularly problematic is the increasing number of working poor. Employment is no longer a guarantee of an adequate wage. Although the number of adults on welfare went up only 14 percent between 1975 and 1986, the number of poor adults who are working rose by 52 percent. This population is not found primarily in our declining inner cities but is scattered across the entire country and is widely distributed among members of all racial and ethnic groups (*U.S. News and World Report*, 1988).

Although this decline in higher paying jobs may be a temporary phenomenon, particularly if projections about a labor shortage in the 1990s prove to be correct, the effects of this deindustrialization of the U.S. economy are not dissimilar to what we might expect following a reduction in economic expansion. The growing level of poverty in the United States is now preventing individuals from securing the basic necessities they and their children need to support their lives. As we either choose or are forced by external circumstances to develop an economy in which the forces of production are contained, we can expect to see this form of hardship and reduced occupational opportunity become more widespread. Such a situation will call into question the viability of capitalism itself; it will also threaten our political structures.

More than 30 years ago, David Potter (1954) argued that democracy, as well as capitalism, may depend upon unlimited economic expansion. The property of the privileged will only remain secure as long as members of the lower classes believe that material conditions are such that they or their descendants may eventually come to share similar privileges. If this situation changes, the poor will become a threat to the rich. The founders of the United States were not insensitive to this dynamic. James Madison, for example, asserted that an ever-expanding empire was essential to ensure the stability of the American government. For two centuries, first an expanding frontier and then an expanding economy have brought to Americans the increasing opportunities required to sustain public faith in the U.S. political and economic systems. If that expansion is curtailed, however, both systems may be jeopardized (Williams, 1980).

Given the limited availability of cheap energy, the curtailment of that expansion is almost a foregone conclusion. With it, we can expect to see a reduction in economic opportunity for an increasing proportion of U.S. workers, a growing rather than declining underclass, threatened democratic institutions, and a continuing erosion of communal safety and civility. In short, changes in our material conditions could precipitate a form of social disintegration not unlike that confronting citizens of the Soviet Union in the final years of the 1980s and the early 1990s. The "triumph of capitalism" may thus be short-lived. The economies of Western nations, richer and more flexible than command economies, could well persist without serious disruption for a number of years. Their ultimate vulnerability to the availability of inexpensive petrochemicals and the environmental consequences of their use, however, cannot be changed. Unless equally cheap but less environmentally damaging energy sources are discovered and widely disseminated within the next sixty years, the efflorescence of productivity that has captured the imaginations of people of the twentieth century will come to an abrupt end, and with it many of the institutions we value most.

We face, at this point in history, a critical moment. If steps are not taken to address these crises, we can expect the collapse of necessary ecological and social systems. Diminishing the consequences of this catastrophe will almost certainly require us to invent a new way of being, both with one another and the planet. If unlimited economic expansion is no longer a possibility, we must find ways to provide for the support of people no longer able to make their way in the world as isolated individuals. We must learn as well, that harming the earth, in the end, harms us and our children. Such lessons and social practices appear to be incompatible with the basic premises of the culture we have inherited and are continuing to bequeath to our young. Given this incompatibility, what is called for is nothing less than the invention of a culture more appropriate for the conditions we now face. As one of the primary transmitters of culture, educators have a grave responsibility to participate in this process.

The Failure of Educators to Acknowledge Changing Conditions

Despite the gravity of these environmental and economic developments, few educators have begun to integrate their implications into their own work. Instead, people in the schools and those who direct, teach, or study them are proceeding as if the reality into which most adults were born earlier in this century will continue. Few publicly question the commonly shared assumptions about unlimited growth and expanding individual opportunities that undergird the schools. This is not to say that environmental concerns have not entered the classroom. Children in schools all over the United States are taught about the effects of pollution, deforestation, or the need for recycling. Environmental education, however, has been relegated to the status of another subject, another part of an already overburdened curriculum. This new discipline has had little if any impact upon the underlying goals and objectives of American education (Stevenson, 1987).

As indicated earlier, the central preoccupation of most educational debate over the previous decade has been America's competitiveness in an international market. This certainly was the motivating factor behind the reform movement in the early 1980s. Among the proposals from this period that received the most attention were *A Nation at Risk: The Imperative for Educational Reform*, by the National Commission on Excellence in Education (1983); *Action for Excellence: A Comprehensive Plan to Improve Our Nation's Schools*, by the Task Force on Education for Economic Growth of the Education Commission of the States (1983); *Academic Preparation for College: What Students Need to Know and Be Able to Do*, by the College Board (1983); and *Making the Grade*, by the Twentieth Century Fund Task Force on Federal Elementary and Secondary Education Policy (1983). Summarizing these proposals, Stedman and Smith (1983) suggest that

Their recommendations are designed to cure our educational failures and to prepare students for a new society—for a future economy based on high technology, emphasizing information processing and computers. By adopting these recommendations, the commissions believe, the United States can recapture its economic vigor and regain its competitive edge in the world economy. (87)

These reports—nearly all of which are politically conservative in orientation—assume that by upgrading content, raising academic standards, increasing time on academic subjects, educating for economic growth, training students in the skills necessary for college, and providing greater incentives and standards for the teaching profession, American schools will be able to develop a work force capable of competing in the international marketplace. That this marketplace may be threatened by limitations imposed by the planet is never acknowledged.

Instead, the reports suggest that what threatens the United States is our unwillingness to demand that American children do more. If only U.S. students and the schools that prepare them produced the level of mastery and commitment encountered abroad, then our former economic preeminence could be regained. The authors of *A Nation at Risk* (1983), for example, see our current predicament in these terms:

Knowledge, learning, information, and skilled intelligence are the new raw materials of international commerce and are today spreading throughout the world as vigorously as miracle drugs, synthetic fertilizers, and blue jeans did earlier. If only to keep and improve the slim competitive edge we still retain in world markets, we must dedicate ourselves to the reform of our educational system for the benefit of all—old and young alike, affluent and poor, majority and minority. Learning is the indispensable investment required for success in the "information" age we are entering. (4)

Furthermore, they go on to suggest that the promise of individual fulfillment through educational attainment remains intact.

All, regardless of race or class or economic status, are entitled to a fair chance and to the tools for developing their individual powers of mind and spirit to the utmost. This promise means that all children by virtue of their own efforts, competently guided, can hope to attain the mature and informed judgment needed to secure gainful employment and to manage their own lives, thereby serving not only their own interests but also the progress of the society as a whole. (5)

In two sentences, the authors of this report articulate the fundamental American faith in the ability of education to advance individual opportunity that environmental developments threaten to contradict and which deindustrialization is currently disproving. If such spokespeople feel any uncertainty about the negative impact that resource depletion or ecological crises may have on the continued health of our economy and social life, they betray none of it in these reports. Their suggestions are a recipe for an intensified continuation of business as usual.

Although highly influential among governmental policy makers, the reform reports of the early 1980s received mixed reactions from the educational community itself, particularly its more liberal members. Most criticism, however, tended to be directed to the authors' faulty use of data or the negative implications of standardization and higher requirements for youth already at risk of educational failure (Kaestle, 1985; McDill, Natriello, and Pallas, 1986; Stedman and Smith, 1983). By the end of the 1980s, the first wave of reform, as it came to be labeled, was replaced by a second that called for more fundamental forms of educational change. Instead of simply intensifying current practice, second wave spokespeople argued that schools needed to be restructured (Council of Chief State School Officers, 1989; David, Purkey, and White 1989; O'Neill, 1990). Only if curriculum and instruction as well as school governance practices were changed would schools be able to adapt to the needs of a postindustrial society. Although second wave reformers brought to the debate a commendable concern for equity as well as excellence, the central motivation behind this movement has remained the preparation of American students for a competitive global market in which continued growth is unquestioned.

In *The Moral and Spiritual Crisis in Education*, Purpel (1989) suggests that the source of this peculiar blindness on the part of contemporary educators is related to their preoccupation with the techniques of schooling. This has led those who study schools or who work in them to disregard their role as the transmitters of cultural values responsible for our current impasse. Instead of dealing with these broader issues, they focus on an increasingly minute analysis of current educational practice. Though the study of curriculum, pedagogy, and school structures has utility and potential merit, it too often distracts people within the schools from the real work at hand, and ignores entirely the role that educators might play in forging a cultural orientation more appropriate for the changed reality that may face our children and grandchildren. To quote Purpel:

> given the elements of our political, economic, and cultural crises, educational discourse must focus on the urgent task of transforming many of our basic cultural institutions and belief systems. Responses that are at best ameliorative have the danger of deepening the crisis by further strengthening social and cultural policies and practices that endanger our deepest commitments. If we accept the basic proposition that we must make some drastic changes in our culture to forestall danger and facilitate growth, then clearly educational institutions must be a part of the process. However energetic and imaginative, efforts that ignore or deny this necessity are eligible for "trivial" status. (3)

Regrettably, much if not most educational research and innovation fails to touch upon the most serious issues of our time.

A similar myopia is demonstrated even by leftist critics of American education. Even though such critics must be commended for their concern regarding the complicity of schools in perpetuating economic discrimination, they rarely look beyond these economistic issues to the ecological context in which they are embedded (Apple, 1982; Bowles and Gintis, 1976, 1986; Carnoy and Levin, 1985). Instead, they turn their attention to questions of distribution, both of resources and power, and the ways in which these might be shared more equitably throughout the entire society. Although the issue of equitable distribution is unquestionably important, little thought is apparently being directed to the possibility that environmental limitations may impose severe restrictions on available resources. Instead, there seems to be a general consensus that the standard of living now enjoyed by the American middle class can somehow be made available to all. Such a vision of the future is undeniably attractive, but the earth itself appears to be incapable of sustaining it.

Educators, regardless of their political persuasion, thus seem unwilling to confront the possibility that modern industrialism will almost certainly be constrained by natural limits, and that such constraints call into question fundamental assumptions about the historical process, progress, and the place of humanity on this planet. Nor is much consideration given to the forms of social relations that may be more appropriate for an emerging reality that, when first recognized, is both frightening and saddening. It seems imperative, however, that we confront both our fear and despair about the changes that are taking place around us in order to guarantee any kind of future for our children. By grappling with that fear and despair we may come to see this difficult era as one which is rich in possibilities as well as dangers.

Reconceiving Education for an Era of Environmental Limits

Just as schools have played a significant role in helping formerly agrarian populations adapt to the opportunities and requirements of the modern world, they might now play a role in midwifing cultural changes necessitated by the requirements presented by the planet's unavoidable material barriers. These barriers may force us to reformulate social relations with a more circumspect and realistic understanding of our own limitations. Educators could offer important guidance as changing material conditions require us to alter our response to the physical environment and one another.

If educators are to play this role, it seems essential at the outset to explore the ways in which current educational practices and policies are inextricably wedded to the worldview that underlies modernization. It is this worldview which has led us to believe that liberating ourselves from our natural and social environments is both desirable and possible. Until this worldview is illuminated and critiqued, and until its relationship to the structures, practices, and curriculum encountered in U.S. schools is understood, it will not be possible to develop new educational forms more appropriate for the limited and interdependent era we are now entering.

Chapter 2 provides a brief overview of the primary components of this worldview. The analysis contained here summarizes the work of other scholars who have sought to unravel the central belief structures or ideology of modernism. Though their interpretations remain subject to debate, they offer a useful means for disentangling why it is we have come to our current situation and what it may take to move on. This chapter should be viewed as a conceptual tool by which we might more fully understand the operation of our schools, and in understanding that operation, transform them.

Chapter 3 focuses on the nature of contemporary education in the United States and the way in which our schools transmit and confirm the conceptual assumptions and social practices of the modern/industrial worldview. Central to the thesis of this book is the claim that schools can play an important role in shaping the habits and attitudes upon which social life is constructed. In an attempt to substantiate this claim, I review the way in which children's adjustments to the behavioral and programmatic regularities of the school (Sarason, 1982) prepare them for participation in the modern world.

Just as an identifiable worldview undergirds current educational practice, so another worldview may need to buttress the educational forms required for life in the economic and social environment that will result from a contraction in the forces of production. Chapter 4 presents the outlines of a worldview that is now emerging in response to the environmental developments discussed earlier. This worldview is associated with a variety of spokespeople, although it is currently being articulated most vocally by radical ecologists and members of environmental movements in a number of advanced industrial nations. It could be argued that this worldview, given its marginality, is unlikely to have any influence on public policy or the shape of public education. Although it is impossible to predict the future, the perspective shared by this loose collection of activists and theoreticians comes closer to acknowledging the cultural, economic, and political implications of the ecological crisis than the worldviews provided by any other group, especially by those on the political right or left. For that reason, I have chosen this perspective as the basis upon which to construct educational practices more appropriate for the reality that may await us.

Chapters 5 and 6 will discuss the implications of this emerging worldview for educational practice. Chapter 5 provides a tentative model of an educational process more likely than the current dominant pattern to affirm children's interconnectedness with one another and the natural environment. This model specifically addresses elements of conventional educational practice that appear to encourage detached independence, achievement, and conformity to bureaucratic categories and regulations. Because such a model runs the risk of being perceived as impractical, Chapter 6 describes a variety of current educational programs that in fact embody many of the principles set out in the previous chapter. These innovations are becoming increasingly widespread throughout public education, especially in alternative educational programs now being created to foster school success and retention for economically or socially disadvantaged students. Few, if any, of these innovations are specifically aimed at instilling the forms of interdependent and participatory social relations that concern me here, particularly as they are aimed toward adaptation to a profoundly altered economic environment. If combined, however, many of these practices could serve as important components of the hypothetical school described in Chapter 5.

The final chapter considers strategies for developing and implementing an educational process more in line with a worldview that recognizes our limitations and inescapable interdependence. Succeeding in such a project would perhaps be hopeless if there were not already widespread dissatisfaction with public education. Tapping into that dissatisfaction may be the most important tactic for establishing alternative forms of educational practice. Doing so will require eliciting the support of three constituencies: governmental, corporate, and educational policymakers; the general public; and public school educators. The process of gaining such support will be inherently contradictory because the goals of the schools described here run counter to the worldview of nearly all sectors of the American public. Conditions are such, however, that proposals which in the past would have been rejected may now be accepted because of the gravity of current problems and their intractability in the face of more conventional solutions. The space exists to foster change; our task is to make use of it.

Two

❖

Modernization and the Rejection of Interdependence

Schools have played a critical role in the dissemination of an interpretation of reality unique to our own era. As indicated earlier, this interpretation or worldview asserts that we as a species can liberate ourselves from restraints imposed by nature and that our domination of the physical world diminishes our need to rely on one another to attain satisfactory levels of personal security. What can be called the modern/industrial worldview contrasts with worldviews encountered in earlier agricultural and other premodern societies in which the embeddedness of our species in natural and social environments was unquestioned. Although this worldview has allowed us to achieve the degree of detached self-consciousness Marx believed was essential if human beings were to manipulate the material world to their own advantage (Cohen, 1978, 10), it is also now threatening the finely tuned cycles and ecosystems of the planet as a whole.

Developing an educational process sensitive to these cycles and ecosystems will require us to examine and understand central premises of the worldview that has brought us to the impasse we are now facing. Without such an examination and understanding, we run the risk of simply reforming schools in ways that will continue to foster habits of thought and behavior that perpetuate our alienation from natural systems and prevent us from developing patterns of mutual support needed to negotiate a world of reduced individual opportunities.

Before embarking on a discussion about the worldview that appears to underlie contemporary American schools, however, it must be acknowledged that such discussions run the risk of superficiality or caricature. Reducing a civilization to a handful of concepts is an exercise that inevitably excludes conflicting evidence and simplifies the complex. The generalizations encountered in this form of discourse also tend to highlight the works of particular seminal thinkers. Ideas, from this perspective, are what shape the world. Despite the dangers of superficiality and an overemphasis on the power of ideas, however, discussions about worldviews can reveal, at least partially, taken-for-granted assumptions that may strongly influence our relations with one another and the world around us. After our physical needs have been met, it is often these mental commitments that shape our actions and personal loyalties.

What follows is a synthesis of different analyses of the dominant Western worldview taken from the works of a number of scholars (Berman, 1981; Bowers, 1987; Capra, 1983; Coates, 1981; Devall, 1980; Galtung,1986; Ignatieff, 1984; Ketcham, 1987; Merchant, 1980; Oliver and Gershman, 1989; Smith, 1982) who have addressed themselves to what might be called the crisis of modernization. Although each has offered his or her own analysis of principles underlying the modern/industrial worldview, together they demonstrate a significant degree of unanimity about what those principles are. These principles include the following:

1. Because the universe is orderly, mechanical, and predictable, the best way to know and understand it is to approach it objectively, utilizing the intellectual tools of rationalism and empiricism. Once we have mastered its mechanical principles, we will become capable of controlling the natural world in ways that advance our own welfare.
2. Society, like the natural world, functions as a machine in which individuals are the basic unit. Individuals can make the greatest contribution to the well-being of society if they are allowed to develop personal talents free from the restrictions imposed by traditional forms of human association.
3. Society, like the natural world, is subject to human control. This control is most effective when societies are centrally organized.
4. Given our ability to understand and control both the natural world and society, humans can anticipate advancing toward ever-increasing levels of material comfort and security.

It is important to acknowledge that most of the scholars who have articulated these principles are critics of modernity who counterpoise their discussion of the modern/industrial worldview against those found in traditional societies or in the society they imagine must take the place of our own after the scientific and industrial revolutions have run their course. Despite their bias, however, their presentation of the tenets of our current worldview has an internal consistency and relevance to our present situation that I have found helpful in understanding how contemporary schools contribute to the forms of social and environmental detachment that seem increasingly counterproductive to our common welfare.[1]

The World Is a Machine That Can Be Mastered by Human Beings

Huston Smith (1982, 7) suggests that underlying modernity is the assumption that the universe possesses an order whose laws of operation are accessible to human understanding. The discoveries of scientists in the sixteenth and seventeenth centuries demonstrated that human reason could reveal the working principles of events formerly regarded as unpredictable and inscrutable. Kepler, for example, following a painstaking analysis of astronomical tables, discovered that the orbits of the planets were subject to mathematical representation and conformed to the heliocentric theory of Copernicus. Through the utilization of systematic forms of experimentation, Galileo likewise demonstrated that the motion of falling bodies conformed to principles subject to human analysis and representation. With his articulation of the law of gravity, Newton provided a conceptual mechanism able to predict the motion of both earthly and celestial bodies. Rather than being viewed as a complex yet unified entity that defied human comprehension, sharing in the mystery of the divine, the universe came to be seen as little more than a complicated machine that, with enough testing and examination, could be clearly described and successfully manipulated.

In contrast, most men and women prior to the modern era viewed the universe not as a series of objects to be tested and used, but as a place of belonging, alive with the same spirit that filled their own bodies (Berman, 1981). Throughout the Middle Ages, for example, Europeans generally saw themselves as participants in a vast cosmic drama in which humanity stood midway between lower creatures and the divine, only one link in an extended chain of beings suffused with interrelated meaning. The world among such people was not an alien and impersonal machine, but a vehicle through which the "whys" of our existence could be grasped. Though the answers to these "whys" remained necessarily metaphorical and inexact, they contributed to the belief encountered in many earlier societies that the universe, despite its pain and suffering, was a place where men and women could feel at home.

After the advent of the modern/industrial worldview, however, the universe was stripped of any transcendental purpose that might have bearing on our spiritual lives, and a god that had once been immanent was removed to the borders of the cosmos. A natural environment that had previously been intimately connected to ourselves was now seen to be only motion and matter, devoid of either purpose or divinity (Berman, 1981). Schiller described this process as *die Entgotterung der Natur*, or the "de-godding" of nature (in Sale, 1985, 16). A century later, Max Weber suggested that the acceptance of a scientific outlook came at the cost of *die Entzauberung der Welt*, or the "disenchantment of the world" (in Berman, 1981, 69).

This alteration of perspective has denied our interrelationship with the world and has led us to believe that we are capable of transcending the limitations of the physical environment by becoming masters of, rather than participants in, its rhythms, patterns, and uncertainties. The assumption of transcendent mastery has been based at least in part on the way in which scientists have chosen to study the physical universe. Given the modern belief that the universe functions as a machine rather than as an interrelated manifestation of the divine, the most plausible way to discover its operational principles lies not in intuitive discernment, mythology, or the interpretive traditions of medieval scholarship, but in the assumption of a posture of detached objectivity (Coates, 1981, 24). Accompanying this objectivity has been a shift of attention away from a contemplation of the whole to an examination of component parts (Oliver and Gershman, 1989). Instead of looking at the natural world as a source of wonder, intellectuals began observing it with the eyes of a mechanical engineer. As Robert Hooke, a seventeenth-century physicist, remarked, the scientific revolution allowed humans "to discover all the secret workings of Nature, almost in the same manner as we do those that are the productions of Art and are manag'd by Wheels, and Engines, and Springs" (in Sale, 1985, 16). With the growing acceptance of the atomic theory and its assertion that the universe was composed of nothing more than inert particles of matter, such a perspective became increasingly acceptable. It also matched the orientation of sixteenth-century artisans, who, thanks to their growing wealth and social influence, were making inroads into traditional scholarship (Berman, 1981, 58). Concerned with the manipulation of matter rather than speculation about its purpose, they had little patience for or interest in the interpretive studies and commentaries of medieval clerics.

Galileo occupied a pivotal position between the old perspective and the new. A university professor, he nevertheless approached his research into the natural world as an artisan, designing experiments in an elaborate workshop to test and retest his hypotheses about motion, material resistance, and other matters that had direct technological applications (Berman, 1981, 61). His methodology expunged subjectivity and a concern for teleological explanations. Galileo was not concerned about the *why* behind phenomena, but only the *how*. He discovered this how by analyzing physical processes not under natural conditions but within the context of carefully crafted experiments designed to break down a physical phenomenon into its constituent parts. In his descriptions of his findings he relied upon the abstract and objective language of mathematics, believing that only numbers were capable of representing truth.

Galileo anticipated and combined the suggestions of two primary theorists of the scientific method: René Descartes and Francis Bacon. Superficially, their methods appear to represent the poles of rationalism and empiricism; this apparent opposition, however, is in practice complementary (Berman, 1981, 36). For Descartes, the senses could not be trusted as a means for discovering truth. Truth was located in the conceptual formulations of the mind. His seminal statement, "I think, therefore I am," represents the kernel of his epistemological position. For Bacon, truth could be known through the senses, but its discovery could only be achieved through the experimental manipulation of the physical world, or as Bacon himself said, by "putting Nature to the rack" (in Smith, 1982, 135) and "vexing her until she revealed her secrets" (in Berman, 1981, 30).

Despite the differences in the methodological perspectives of these two men, each argued that the discovery of truth required us to step back from the material world and to treat it as essentially other. In his representation of observed phenomenon through mathematical symbols and his utilization of contrived experiments to test his hypotheses, Galileo juxtaposed the detachment of both rationalism and empiricism and opened the door to the scientific revolution.

In opening that door, however, Galileo and other proponents of this new epistemology challenged the authenticity of our common, unmediated experience. If light objects fall as rapidly as heavy ones, if the earth navigates the sun rather than the reverse, if matter is in actuality empty space, then of what value are our own sensory perceptions? From a scientific viewpoint, such data are of limited utility.

What is required is the acquisition of the proper conceptual tools, perspectives, and expertise. No longer could the knowledge of the untutored be trusted. Although the perspective of science has brought with it a more complete understanding of the operation of physical reality, it has also tended to divorce human beings from their own encounters with the world. According to the modern/industrial worldview, then, personal knowledge is of limited significance, as is personal experience. Despite its immediacy and apparent authenticity, such knowledge lacks the generalizability and predictability of scientific knowledge. Reality is only encountered as we detach ourselves from lived experience and examine it with intellectual tools that lead not to holistic participation but to an objective analysis of its component parts.

Few of the early exponents of modernity, however, considered this shift from a participatory to a detached form of consciousness to be problematic. They were consumed instead with the potentialities of control and prediction that this new approach to knowledge might bring. Descartes, in his *Discourse on Method*, states:

> [My discoveries] have satisfied me that it is possible to reach knowledge that will be of much utility in this life; and that instead of the speculative philosophy now taught in the schools we can find a practical one, by which, knowing the nature and behavior of fire, water, air, stars, the heavens, and all the other bodies which surround us, as well as we now understand the different skills of our workers, we can employ these entities for all the purposes for which they are suited, and so make ourselves masters and possessors of nature. (in Berman, 1981, 25)

Those who share this viewpoint tend to see the natural world as a repository of resources available for human use. Max Weber noted that when objects are viewed as isolated entities rather than as part of an embracing and yet transcendental context, all that is left is their utility. He called this attitude of mind *zweckrational*, which means "purposive or instrumental rationality" (Berman, 1981, 40). From this perspective, things have meaning only insofar as they are profitable or expedient for us.

The aim of most scientific inquiry is thus radically different from intellectual activity prior to our own time. The discovery of meaning is no longer seen as primary; what is sought instead is the ability to predict and then control, and it is those intellectual disciplines that facilitate prediction and control which receive recognition and reward. At base, the knowledge that is valued most in the modern era is the knowledge of artisans, the knowledge that allows us to shape the natural environment in whatever way we wish. In a sense, the scientific revolution has turned the entire world into a workshop in which all phenomena are judged on the basis of their usefulness rather than upon the simple fact of their existence. Coates (1981) summarizes this tenet of the modern/industrial mindset in the following way:

> It is believed that the domination of nature is both necessary and desirable, since nature is just so much undeveloped raw "stuff" to be used for human ends. Human beings are the end and purpose of evolution, and only people, as self-conscious beings, can be considered fully alive. (25)

Our celebration of knowledge for utility and control, however, has led over time to the erosion of other forms of knowledge. Huston Smith (1982) suggests that lost in this process has been what he calls the perennial wisdom, found in nearly all traditions, that emphasizes our interdependence with rather than domination of the natural world. It has been these traditions that have sustained our species for millennia. Neither Bacon nor Descartes, however, had any patience for such old ways. Bacon wrote, for example,

> [It] is idle to expect any great advancement in science from the superinducing and engrafting of new things upon old. We must begin anew from the very foundations, unless we would revolve forever in a circle with mean and contemptible progress. (in Berman, 1981, 29)

And Descartes observed, "As far as the opinions which I had been receiving since my birth were concerned, I could not do better than to reject them completely for once in my life time...." (in Berman, 1981, 32). For both men, the beginning point at which true knowledge could be attained was a radical and methodical doubt about all traditions inherited from the past. Ketcham (1987) notes the corrosive impact of this perspective on all previous forms of knowledge:

> Bacon's inductive method required individuals (any number of them; singly or in groups; the more the better) to gather data, assiduously and endlessly, in order to frame hypotheses that other individuals would then test by gathering more data, in order to posit new hypotheses, *ad infinitum*. The implicit assumption was that there were no final truths imposed on the

human race from above, or anywhere else, but rather that the parts, ultimately individuals in their particular endeavors, were of the essence. In laborious, multitudinous, minute, critical inquiries, Bacon asserted, humankind would find the knowledge that was power over nature itself: "the true and lawful goal of the sciences is none other than this: that human life be endowed with new discoveries and powers...." Powerful intellectual tools had been fashioned that allowed critical analysis to devastate dogma and ancient systems. (55)

In a fundamental way, then, the modern/industrial worldview has led to our detachment from a sense of participatory relatedness to the natural environment, from our own concrete experience of that environment, and from the collective wisdom about how to interact with that environment inherited from our ancestors. In saying this, however, I do not mean to suggest that the modern proclivity to step away from our experience of the physical universe should be completely abandoned. A degree of detachment, as Marx observed, is essential if we are to reflect and act upon our circumstances. The danger in our own era has arisen from our tendency to conflate intellectual detachment with the possibility of actually liberating ourselves from our fundamental embeddedness in the physical matrix of our own existence. Adopting a position of detached objectivity in an attempt to master nature, we have tended to forget our fundamental connection to the world we observe. In failing to recognize this identification, many of us, until recently, have generally overlooked the destructive consequences of the creativity and growth unleashed by the scientific and industrial revolutions.

Some of the costs of this alienation from physical reality were discussed earlier. If we are to reduce or eliminate phenomena such as acid rain, the depletion of the ozone layer, the exhaustion of fossil fuel reserves and forests, or the pollution of land and water, what will be required is not merely the invention of new forms of technical control, but a recollection of our ineluctable embeddedness within the natural world. We must recognize that despite our ability to uncover some of the operating principles of matter and motion, this capacity does not alter the basic facts of our own and the earth's limitations. We remain dependent on soil and air and water for our very existence. These resources, we are now discovering, are inescapably finite. Furthermore, as we damage them, we injure ourselves.

Recognizing the danger of the modern/industrial belief that human beings can sustain a position of detached mastery of the natural world, however, will not be enough to correct the grave ecological problems currently facing us. Our detachment from what some have called the community of all beings has been paralleled by a detachment from human communities as well. This latter form of detachment has contributed to a preoccupation with individual security and well-being that has been one of the primary engines of modern development and could be one of the primary impediments to a restoration of sustainable economic and environmental practices. As long as the residents of industrialized countries continue to believe that their survival is a purely individual rather than a collective responsibility, it is likely that they will seek to guarantee their own well-being and self-interest regardless of the broader social or ecological damage caused by their actions (Hardin, 1968; Banfield, 1958).

Society Is a Machine in Which Individuals Are the Moving Parts

Sale (1985) and Berman (1981) suggest that the epistemological stance proposed by the exponents of the scientific revolution achieved rapid and widespread acceptance because it so closely matched the needs of the market economy and nation states emerging at the same time. Sale admits that this interrelationship is complex, but goes on to indicate that

> it is easy enough to see that certain aspects of the new science would be welcomed by the established powers of the time: the celebration of the mechanical, the tangible, the quantifiable, the utilitarian, the linear, and the divisible, as against the organic, the spiritual, the incalculable, the mysterious, the circular, and the holistic. For the new *nationalism* that wished to establish its control over all secular matters by immutable laws and to regard its denizens as measurable and manipulable objects, and for the new *capitalism* that wished to oversee the materialistic and impersonal marketplace and to develop and exploit the new-found colonial territories, the underlying principles of the scientific ideology were obviously ideal. (19)

Berman similarly notes that modern science provides the "mental framework of a world defined by capital accumulation" (1981, 49). In both science and capitalism, mathematics is the language of choice; in both as well, quantification is the route to personal success, either in terms of the discovery of scientific truth or the mastery of the marketplace (55). Finally, both money and mathematics are "neutral." Without content, they can be bent to any purpose in a world ripe for human exploitation and development (56).

It is not surprising, therefore, that scientific theories regarding the nature of matter and motion came to influence the thinking of those whose attention was directed not to physical phenomena but to human society. Drawing upon the scientific assertion that the universe is composed of atoms (or corpuscles), Thomas Hobbes (1651/1962) argued that society is made up of individuals who, like the particles that constitute matter, are discrete, independent, and in constant motion. Propelled by their desire for self-preservation, human beings possess no underlying relationship with one another and care only about their own survival and the power they are able to establish over others (MacPherson 1962, 45).

Hobbes believed, however, that outside the context of society, such survival is precarious. Competition for scarce resources makes life in the state of nature "solitary, poor, nasty, brutish, and short." He hypothesized that humans, recognizing the liability of this mode of existence, formed society as a means for self-protection. By contracting with an external ruler who would be given absolute authority to prevent any person from impinging upon the activities of another, individuals could continue to pursue their own self-interest free from the fear that others might interfere with them. Hobbes saw such relations, like the interrelationships encountered in the natural world, as purely instrumental, requiring no reference to a hierarchy of moral values or teleological principles (MacPherson, 1962, 17). Hobbes thus stripped society of meaning or value in the same way that physical scientists stripped the natural world of meaning as they sought to manipulate and exploit it.

C. B. MacPherson (1962) suggests that behind this analysis lay not an investigation of a cross-section of societies but Hobbes's experience of a new form of social relations based upon participation in a market economy, a phenomenon that had emerged during the late Middle Ages and had come to dominate European life. Within this context,

> The individual was seen neither as a moral whole, nor as part of a larger social whole, but as an owner of himself. The relation of ownership, having become for more and more men the critically important relation determining their actual freedom and actual prospect of realising their full potentialities, was read back into the nature of the individual. The individual, it was thought, is free inasmuch as he is proprietor of his person and capacities.

The human essence is freedom from dependence on the wills of others, and freedom is a function of possession. Society becomes a lot of free equal individuals related to each other as proprietors of their own capacities and of what they have acquired by their exercise. Society consists of relations of exchange between proprietors. Political society becomes a calculated device for the protection of this property and for the maintenance of an orderly relation of exchange. (3)

In this summary statement about market relations and their influence upon the political analysis of Hobbes, MacPherson articulates a cogent and provocative description of the possessive (in terms of owning and selling one's own capacities) individualism and centralization that are characteristic of modern society. This and the following section will consider these principles in more detail.

In Hobbes's state of nature, individuals are seen as independent of any other forms of human association. They are isolated actors in an economic arena where their worth and support can be determined upon the basis of what they own and/or the skills they possess. What is seen in this hypothetical state of nature is the individualism that has become one of the dominant ideologies of our own era. As Ketcham (1987) defines it,

individualism takes the single person as the self-evident starting point for considering the nature and purposes of social life. Society is not thought of as having an organic life of its own that might make legitimate demands on individuals beyond those accepted voluntarily for the necessity and convenience of living in proximity to other human beings.... Each person is preoccupied with individual survival, success, and satisfactions. (x)

This type of interrelationship between the individual and the broader society, though it occurs on occasion in earlier civilizations among elite classes (Sagan, 1985), never became widespread until the advent of modernization. Prior to the economic expansion that occurred at the close of the European Middle Ages, most human beings lived in communities where the group rather than the individual was seen as the fundamental unit; individual identity grew out of this social matrix rather than the reverse. Alasdair MacIntyre (1981) notes that

In many pre-modern, traditional societies it is through his or her membership of [sic] a variety of social groups that the individual identifies himself or herself and is identified by others. I am brother, cousin and grandson, member of this household, that village, this tribe.... Individuals inherit a particular space within an interlocking set of social relationships; lacking that space, they are nobody, or at best a stranger or an outcast. (32)

In the context of the marketplace, traditionally the site where strangers rather than intimates came to exchange goods (Sahlins, 1965) membership in specific groups becomes less meaningful. This leads to a situation in which individuals are defined not by their relationships to specific people or to a specific place but by the materials or the skills they can offer for sale to others. An individual's worth or power is calculated on the basis of two things: first, by the excess personal capacities he or she can display over those displayed by others, and secondly, by what he or she can acquire as a result of that excess (MacPherson, 1962, 35). The individual in such a situation becomes a commodity whose value is judged by his or her utility to others. Personal worth is no longer grounded in social identity, but tied to the comparative value of one individual against another. In this situation, survival depends on competition with strangers rather than cooperation with intimates.

This commodification of the individual was encouraged by other trends that were altering the nature of production and commerce during the same period. With the growth of the textile trade in Northern Europe, entrepreneurs sought to break through the constraints on individual profit imposed by the medieval guild system by transplanting the manufacturing process from towns to the countryside. Rural peasants, supplied with looms and thread, were paid wages for their labor. Their wages, however, did not carry the promise of economic support that had once been part of manorial life. Labor was entered into on a contractual rather than a moral basis. Compensation was limited to payment for services provided. As international trade blossomed during this era, the authority of the guilds was further eroded, and wage labor became more widespread.

With the industrial revolution in the eighteenth and nineteenth centuries, wage labor became the dominant economic relationship as factories displaced the productive role once played by the family. From this time up to the present, an increasing number of individuals have been thrust into an economic environment where they are forced to compete with strangers for their own support. In answer to this competition, individuals have sought to develop themselves as human products capable of surviving the rigors of the marketplace

(Steinetz and Solomon, 1986). This is one of the reasons that education has played an increasingly important role in modern/industrial societies (Church and Sedlak, 1976). Through formal schooling, individuals gain the training they need to present themselves as more capable and skilled in an environment where the possession of desirable attributes and abilities is a requirement for economic security.

As individuals have come to acquire these attributes and abilities and as the labor market has continued to absorb them, earlier forms of economic interdependence and cooperation have become less compelling. It has also been increasingly assumed that individuals are responsible for themselves alone and not for the communities in which they live. The able and mature are expected to construct independent rather than interdependent lives for themselves. Those who fail to make their way in this competitive and demanding economic environment are seen to be spiritually, morally, or intellectually deficient (Sennett and Cobb, 1972). Few realize that this form of social interpretation is in itself an ideological construction, reflecting not reality but an unquestioned acceptance of one of the primary tenets of the modern/industrial worldview.

The belief that society is composed of unrelated individuals whose only reason for association is the protection of self-interest has undercut the authority of broader social meanings. As the marketplace has increasingly usurped the place of institutions such as the church or family, our society has been robbed of the *telos*, or purpose, encountered in previous civilizations. Without it, there is no ground upon which to base concepts of personal or social morality (MacIntyre, 1981). From the mid-nineteenth century on, social critics such as Nietzsche and Dostoyevsky have warned that this process could bring with it a drift into nihilism and amorality capable of destroying human society. Without a shared vision of moral goodness or excellence, all that will link men and women to one another will be relations of power and domination. As Max Horkheimer has observed: "In the course of emancipation man shares the fate of his world: domination of nature implies social domination" (in Dallmayr, 1981, 10). As modernization has progressed, moral systems that evolved over millennia have been forgotten or made the object of personal choice rather than obligation.

Our belief in the primacy of the individual has also served to detach us from the forms of obligation and support characteristic of primordial human associations. As Tonnies (1955) noted a century ago, these associations display an intimate solidarity that has become increasingly absent with the spread of a market society. Though supportive, such relations have also traditionally inhibited the scope of personal choice so valued in our own society. In reaction to these inhibitions, individuals in the industrialized West have come to believe that their rights take precedence over communal obligations. Increasingly, they have rejected former patterns of mutuality in preference for greater personal freedom when the possibility of economic independence has allowed them to do so.

In his study of popular individualism, Gans (1988) argues that the history of the United States is a chronicle of the dissolution of traditional forms of social membership and support. This dissolution, already set in motion by the development of a market society in Europe, was encouraged by access to the vast natural resources of the North American continent. Later, industrial development freed people even further from the forms of economic dependency characteristic of earlier societies. The combination of ideology and economic opportunity has thus contributed to the fragmentation of previously cohesive communities into the detached social atoms of a competitive market society.

Finally, individualism, despite its association with democratic forms of governance, has contributed to an increasing withdrawal from civic participation and a diminished concern for the common good. This, in part, has occurred as control over critical elements of our own lives has been shifted to centralized organizations often distant from the immediate realm of our own responsibilities (Vidich and Bensman, 1968); I explore this issue in more detail in the following section. Reduced citizen participation in public affairs can also be tied to the role ascribed to government in a market society. According to the political theories of Hobbes and Locke, theories that lie behind the constitutions of most Western democracies, governments should exercise no positive function; they should simply guard the public peace, allowing individuals to pursue their own material interests as long as they threaten neither their fellows nor the State (Hobbes 1651/1962, 161; Nisbet, 1973, 142). Ketcham emphasizes this issue in his study, *Individualism and Public Life: A Modern Dilemma* (1987). There he states:

> Once politics is defined negatively, that is, seen as a means merely for protecting or enhancing private interests, then explicit public concerns become secondary or even nonexistent. Citizens of such a negatively defined entity, habituated to see even their own democratic government as a problem, will tend to blame it for troublesome intrusions, to see public-spirited initia-

tives as masks for self-interests, and to absolve themselves of any responsibility for the inadequacies, frustrations, and injustices of the nation's common life. (viii)

Within this context, the health of the commonwealth becomes a secondary concern. Particularly as people imagine that their well-being is not tied to the lives of others beyond their immediate circle, it becomes easy to believe that society has no "organic life of its own that might make legitimate demands on individuals beyond those accepted voluntarily for the necessity and convenience of living in proximity to other human beings" (Ketcham, 1987, x); failing to recognize the "organic life" of society, individuals can then act as though the commonweal will take care of itself.

Attention is then directed toward maintaining and furthering individual security. Gans (1988) suggests that it is the attainment of this security, more than convenience or comfort or self-centeredness, that is the aim of individualism. With the knowledge that he or she is in control of the surrounding environment, the individual is then free "to lay the groundwork for self-development" (2). Laying the groundwork for self-development, however, can be dangerously myopic.

This narrow-sightedness is clearly evident in undergraduate responses to a Carnegie Commission survey published in 1981 (Levine, 1981). When asked about the condition of the world, most respondents spoke of social and economic disintegration. When questioned about their own lives, however, the same students expressed optimism about their futures. Their confidence was a product of their belief that graduating from a good college and finding a well-paying job would insulate them from broader social events. They had become so detached from the life of the entire society that they believed they were immune from its maladies. Such detachment bodes ill for the forms of collective action that may be required of us in the coming years.

To summarize, a central premise of the modern era is that society is composed of isolated individuals whose central preoccupation is the pursuit of their own development and economic self-interest. Rather than being seen as members of smaller human associations, members of contemporary societies, particularly in the West, are thought of as independent agents responsible for achieving their own security as a result of successfully participating in a competitive labor market. Larger communal responsibilities and obligations have over time been given less credence, perhaps in part because communities themselves have become less willing to ensure the security of their members. Although this shift in the relationship between the individual and the community has been more or less workable during an era of economic expansion, this view of social reality will be inappropriate if a reduction in the forces of production prevents a majority of citizens from achieving the development they desire. In such a situation, the pursuit of self-interest could bring with it security for the few rather than the many, a recipe not for individual freedom but tyranny.

Centralization: Ordering the Lives of Detached Individuals

Accompanying the modern era's emphasis on individualism has been an equally important expansion of centralized control over our political and economic lives, a process that has also furthered the dissolution of smaller human associations, diminishing their authority and ability to address fundamental human needs. Through this process, individuals have been detached not only from one another and the social whole but also from the power and efficacy they once achieved through local and regional forms of collective action.

Prior to the modern era, European governments were interested in exercising only minimal regulatory control over the activities of their citizens. Social order and production were maintained largely as a result of customary practices encountered in local communities. Towns and villages were essentially self-governing and self-sufficient, and children learned the skills required to support themselves and pay taxes from their parents or neighbors.

With the development of a nonlocal market society, however, new forms of social competition threatened the order that had previously been maintained in a less centralized manner. Where before, feudal patterns of economic dependency and obligation had regulated social and political interactions, the proliferation of a class freed from such dependency required the development of a new form of governance. In response to such changes, political theorists looked to the only political organization capable of imposing order upon an expanding market society, the nation state. Intentionally or not, they took as a model of reform the market itself.

Traditionally, markets provided a place where violence between members of antagonistic groups was proscribed in the interest of furthering the safe exchange of goods (Kropotkin, 1914/1972; Sahlins, 1965). As indicated earlier, within the market individuals interacted with one another not on the basis of communal ties and obligations but in accordance with commonly agreed-upon rules. Such rules were temporarily sovereign and took precedence over other forms of authority or obligation. Finally, people who chose to participate in the marketplace did so of their own free choice, essentially entering into a contractual agreement with its rules in order to gain the opportunity to sell and buy goods.

What was needed during the era of civil and religious wars that wracked Europe in the 1600s was a set of principles by which the authority of the market might be transposed to the level of the State. The rediscovery of the Roman legal code provided a means by which this extension of centralized political control might be achieved (Nisbet, 1973, 121–23). Roman law displays four principles that parallel the nature of political authority encountered in the market. These principles include sovereignty, concession, contract, and the belief that individuals are the primary unit of society. According to the principle of *sovereignty*, political power is preeminent and stands above all other forms of authority, including kinship and religion. The doctrine of *concession* suggests that lesser authority or forms of human association can exist in society only so long as they acknowledge their dependence on centralized political authority. The principle of *contract* asserts that no relations are legal unless they are entered into volitionally, a principle that effectively weakens the authority of all traditional or hereditary forms of relationship. Finally, the consequence of the three preceding principles is that the only remaining unit in society that cannot be dissolved by the sovereign is the individual.

These principles, like the principles of the marketplace, are aimed at reducing the importance of communal ties that might interfere with the social and economic intercourse of strangers. They lead to the detachment of individuals from the intimate forms of authority encountered in the family and small community and assert the authority of officials invested with power by the State. Nisbet (1973, 54) suggests that the creation of national armies may have provided an organizational model by which this form of impersonal and centralized authority could be extended to the body politic. Armies were among the first large organizations to adopt hierarchical chains of command and a wage labor system, innovations that dispensed with the forms of personal allegiance that had been fundamental in feudal militias. Although military organizations during the Roman Empire displayed comparable features, it was only in the late Middle Ages that armies once again were composed of paid mercenaries, subject not to the charismatic authority described in medieval accounts of warfare but to the bureaucratic authority encountered in modern

institutions. Such organizations mirror the universality and imper-
sonality of the market and demonstrate how commercial relations can
be transformed into more static and less fluid institutional structures.

Through the conjunction of national laws and the development
of state bureaucracies civic order was reestablished. This process,
however, was not automatic. Participation in nonintimate, bureaucratic organizations required that citizens be trained to accept the
authority and governance of strangers. In his exploration of discipline
and social control in modern societies, Foucault (1977) offers one
interpretation of how this goal was achieved. Like Nisbet, he points to
the military as the site where this new form of disciplinary training
was initially developed.

> By the late eighteenth century, the soldier has become some-
> thing that can be made; out of a formless clay, an inapt body, the
> machine required can be constructed; posture is gradually cor-
> rected; a calculated constraint runs slowly through each part of
> the body, mastering it, making it pliable, ready at all times, turn-
> ing silently into the automatism of habit; in short, one has 'got
> rid of the peasant' and given him 'the air of a soldier.' (135)

Central to this process was the development of what Foucault
calls *disciplinary power*.

> The basic goal of disciplinary power was to produce a human
> being who could be treated as a "docile body." The docile body
> also had to be a productive body. The technology of discipline
> developed and was perfected in workshops, barracks, prisons,
> and hospitals; in each of these settings the general aim was a
> "parallel increase in the usefulness and docility" of individuals
> and populations. The techniques for disciplining bodies were
> applied mainly to the working classes and the subproletariat,
> although not exclusively, as they also operated in universities
> and schools. (Dreyfus and Rabineau, 1982, 128)

According to Foucault, the application of this disciplinary power has
involved the transmission of "meticulous, often minute" behaviors
and gestures required for the smooth operation of larger social and
economic machinery. It works by approaching the body as an object
to be analyzed and then broken down into its constituent parts. Once
this has been accomplished, the body can then be "subjected, used,
transformed and improved" (Foucault, 1977, 136). Discipline operates

not by "crushing [bodies] or lecturing them, but by 'humble' proce-dures of training and distribution" (Dreyfus and Rabineau, 1982, 156).

Those who are inducted into such training are often unaware of the way in which they are being shaped for participation in large institutions. Such shaping, itself, may even appear advantageous to the individual, since mastering disciplinary techniques brings with it institutional commendations and the promise of economic rewards. By learning to manipulate one's body in the manner desired by the larger society, one is able to increase one's value as a commodity and improve one's chances of individual survival. This, for example, is one of the primary rationales for the acceptance of schooling. Through such a process, individualism and centralization are con-joined.

A new pattern of dependency is thus created, only in this case between individuals and impersonal authority rather than among individuals within intimate groups. Within this broader context, per-sonal power and influence count for significantly less than they do within smaller human associations. Individuals become effectively detached from their own capacity to act with others in ways that might better guarantee their own well-being. Compliance with the dictates and "normalizing judgments" of centralized authority thus becomes virtually essential for survival. In this way, modern societies have been able to extend their power, diminishing the importance of primary groups, yet achieving control over individuals now freed from the obligations once imposed by family and community. As Christopher Lasch (1977, 169) has noted, this detachment from inti-macy and personal power has generally seemed an acceptable price to pay for the material advances that have accompanied the dissemi-nation of the principles of individualism and centralization.

The Promise of Progress and Personal Security

In many respects, faith in material progress has undergirded the extraordinary expansion of the forces of production that has occurred over the previous four centuries. This belief is a new phenomenon. Prior to the scientific and then industrial revolutions, human beings imagined that the suffering and uncertainty of their lives were given. There was no way to circumvent fate in a physical universe controlled by forces and events inaccessible to human reason. Rather than believe they were capable of altering what appeared to be ineluctable, people turned to stoicism, divine intervention, or the possibility of improved circumstances after death. With the successful extension of the power of reason, however, the residents of the modern world no longer needed to rely upon the supernatural for their salvation or wait until death to experience comfort or security. With intelligence, diligence, and commitment they could take salvation into their own hands and create heaven themselves.

Whereas early scientific thinkers such as Descartes or Newton had no intention of challenging the religious doctrines of their own time, by the eighteenth century the philosophers of the French Enlightenment dispensed with God altogether and imagined the possibility of redemption in purely secular terms. Through wise management and planning, they argued, human beings were capable of governing not only the natural world but their own affairs in ways that would eliminate scarcity and our need for "spiritual self-deception" (Ignatieff, 1984, 100). This seeking for secular redemption has been one of the central motivations behind the entire experiment of modernity.

The two primary prophets of this form of redemption have been Adam Smith and Karl Marx. Building upon the individualism identified by Hobbes as fundamental to human society, Smith argued that the pursuit of self-interest was a means for advancing the common good. In doing so he challenged the religious and moral teachings of his own as well as most other societies. He was adamant, however, in his assertion that individuals know best how to meet their own economic needs and should be allowed to do so with the fewest constraints possible. In this way, they would seek their own economic advantage, increase overall productivity and the wealth of the society, and thereby contribute not only to their own welfare but to the welfare of all. Although this process would lead to an inequitable distribution of wealth, the end result would be an amelioration of economic conditions for everyone. Smith described his reasoning in the following passage from his *Theory of Moral Sentiments*:

> The rich only select from the heap what is most precious and agreeable. They consume little more than the poor, and in spite of their natural selfishness and rapacity, though they mean only their own conveniency, though the sole end which they propose from the labours of all the thousands whom they employ, be the gratification of their own vain and insatiable desires, they divide with the poor the produce of all their improvements. They are led by an invisible hand to make nearly the same distribution of the necessities of life, which would have been made, had the earth been divided into equal portions among all its inhabitants, and thus without intending it, without knowing it, advance the

interest of society, and afford means to the multiplication of the species. (in Ignatieff, 1982, 112)

The competitive and impersonal characteristics of the marketplace and the industrial system that supports it therefore become acceptable and even necessary. "Only a society of strangers, of mediated and indirect social relations, has the dynamism to achieve progress" (Ignatieff, 1982, 119).

Smith, again echoing Hobbes, also recognized that the process of economic growth, like the competition for resources and power among individuals, could not be left purely to chance. Above this interaction of increasingly free agents must be an authority capable of moderating the social fragmentation caused by the division of labor. Such an authority must also prevent the injury of one group by another. Smith, for example, placed great faith in the capacity of state-supported education to transmit common beliefs capable of maintaining civic virtue and social order (Ignatieff, 1982, 120). He also believed that governments, through constitutional means, could influence the level of economic productivity among their citizens.

In *The Wealth of Nations*, he distinguished between the experience of the American colonies, with their English constitution, and the colonies in the East Indies dominated and exploited by mercantilist corporations. In the former, individuals were protected by their government and provided with opportunities to earn more than a subsistence wage. The comparatively high standard of living in North America contributed to the strengthening of labor, population growth, and an overall increase in national wealth as a result of individual motivation and initiative. In the East Indies, on the other hand, the ungoverned exploitation of the indigenous population resulted in general impoverishment (Smith, 1947, 391).

What is clear from Smith's illustration is his belief that one form of governance is more appropriate than another in fostering economic development. Like a machine, societies can be operated in one way or another. It is the job of governors to oversee the mode of operation most likely to lead to the forms of political order and economic distribution that will result in the greatest increase in national wealth.

Karl Marx did not question the efficacy of the capitalistic system described and advanced by Smith. He saw the dehumanization and exploitation perpetuated by a market society as an essential stage in the evolution of the forces of production. Only through the liberation of human beings from feudal and superstitious restrictions could their creative energy be released in ways that would bring about the technological innovations required to escape the necessity of labor. As G. A. Cohen points out,

> Despite its consequences for the producers capitalism was need-
> ed for progress, since it extended man's dominion over nature
> and so brought forward the day when the struggle with nature
> could be ended, and so, too, the derivative battle of class against
> class. Only in capitalist organization could the enormous accu-
> mulation of productive power required for liberation be con-
> ceived and achieved. (1980, 25)

The flaw in capitalism, according to Marx, is that the social relations it perpetuates will eventually become inappropriate in a world where the proletariat is no longer needed to produce but only to consume the output of a highly automated system of production.

Both Smith and Marx, therefore, imagined an unlimited vista of material progress that eventually would transform the earth into a virtual paradise where, freed from material scarcity, humans would no longer need to struggle against either nature or one another. As Ignatieff notes, the communist utopia is the fulfillment of the Enlight-enment dream of secular redemption (1982, 100). In some respects, it might also be said to be the fulfillment of the capitalist dream of secu-lar redemption as well, a dream in which all people have been given the leisure and freedom of aristocrats (Cohen, 1978, 324).

As the epistemological tenets of the modern/industrial world-view have detached us from the reality of our embeddedness in the natural environment, and the principles of the market society have detached us from our relatedness to one another, so the ideology of progress, both in its capitalist and socialist forms, has tended to detach us from the inevitability of suffering and our own mortality. We have become accustomed to believing that we are capable of dis-pensing with pain or disease or hunger, and that the continued exis-tence of these phenomena is the result of human ignorance or cupidi-ty. With proper administration, such suffering can be eliminated. But death, of course, cannot be eliminated, and modernity has as yet pro-vided no answer to its finality. Instead of helping us to deal with this eventuality, however, the glitter of the modern world distracts us from what in other cultures has been a primary human task: growth into maturity and wisdom in the face of the unknown. This distrac-tion, which fails to protect us from our fate, nevertheless has served to weaken our identification with the suffering and death of other species, to say nothing of the planet. In our attempt to save ourselves, we have neglected the paths of acceptance and identification that have played such important roles in the evolution of earlier cultures more successful in living harmoniously with the natural environment. We have instead continued to believe that we can somehow stand above the process of life and death; in our hubris, we face our own end as an affront rather than an opportunity.

It may be this form of detachment, and the pride that lies behind it, which is most dangerous and damaging to the natural and human communities that surround us. Failing to grapple honestly with our own mortality, we have ignored the fragility of the lives of other beings. We enter into acts of destruction, thinking that nothing will happen to us. Like the college students surveyed by the Carnegie Foundation, we believe that society can collapse around the perimeter of our lives and we will not be affected. In our steel and concrete cities, in our carpeted and well-heated homes, many of us have attempted to insulate ourselves from suffering and death. In cutting ourselves off from their reality, however, we have forgotten what the sustenance of life requires.

Few premodern communities have been allowed such luxury. For them, a failure to recognize the possibility of death could lead to grave social consequences. Great care was therefore taken to ensure that the land and its spirits were properly attended to and appeased. Ritual practices and taboos governed the use of natural resources, preventing their exhaustion and spoilation. In this way, our ancestors maintained sustainable ecological and economic practices and thus guaranteed their survival. Closer to death, such peoples recognized their intimate relationship with the lives and deaths of others. As we have protected ourselves from that reality, we have assumed the prerogatives of gods. We are now discovering, however, that those prerogatives may have been short-lived indeed.

Moving Beyond a Dysfunctional Worldview

There is no question that these fundamental principles of the modern/industrial worldview have contributed to an extraordinary burst of human creativity and power that has immeasurably improved the lives of millions of people.[2] Though the adoption of this worldview has required us to detach ourselves from surrounding natural and social environments, the benefits of modernization, at least for a sizeable proportion of the residents of the Northern Hemisphere, have appeared more desirable than the forms of belonging and participation encountered in many previous societies. In an ideal world, one might hope that the technological advances which have accompanied the dissemination of this worldview might continue uninterrupted. Our situation, however, is not ideal. Resources necessary to industrial productivity are limited, and we are learning to our surprise that the natural environment is considerably more sensitive to human activities than the architects of modernity had imagined. As a result, we may not be able to persist on our present course without jeopardizing both our own lives and those of future human generations. Changing that course, however, may demand the adoption of a more realistic worldview.

Doing so will require challenging many of our fundamental assumptions about the relationship between the individual and society. Currently, for example, we expect children to view themselves as capable of shaping their lives to their own requirements. We tell them that they have the ability to develop themselves in whatever way they wish. Furthermore, we expect them to pursue this end by detaching themselves economically, if not ideologically, from the families and communities from which they came and to compete in an employment market in which individual worth is measured on the basis of the possession of identifiable talents, skills, and dispositions. Finally, we expect them to believe that this market is implicitly fair, and that the deserving gain appropriate rewards for their attributes. As a society, we assume that by following a course based upon such expectations, a majority of citizens will successfully attain a satisfactory level of material security.

For over 200 years, Americans have had little cause to question the validity of this assumption. With an expanding frontier and then an expanding economy, many individuals with talent and motivation have been able to create moderately secure lives for themselves without relying on the aid of kin group or community for their support.[3] Now, however, we are beginning to find that the earth itself is no longer able to tolerate such a project, whether it be our own or that of other nations. The individual opportunity, security, and freedom we had once assumed might proliferate without end now appear to be finite. Even the security of the privileged will be jeopardized by global warming, ozone depletion, and environmental contamination. Given this situation, a view of reality grounded in cooperation and identification rather than competition and individual detachment may need to be invented, or more accurately, reshaped, if we hope to avoid widespread human misery and the possibility of civil chaos.

In the chapters that follow, I argue that educators, as important disseminators of culture and social relations, have a fundamental obligation to begin to develop and transmit a worldview more appropriate to our changed material conditions. Doing so, however, will require that we acknowledge the degree to which contemporary schools have fostered the confirmation and transmission of the modern/industrial worldview. Despite spoken goals of cultural unification, it has been largely for participation in a competitive market society that public education has prepared our children. Cooperation, participation, and equity, though given lip service, are generally belied by the social relations students encounter in their day-to-day activities in school. By understanding the relationship between contemporary education and a worldview that now appears to be outdated, we will become more able to imagine forms of socialization and cultural transmission more likely to reverse the alienation and detachment of our own era and to foster the collective rather than individual security that will be demanded by a contraction of the forces of production.

Three

❖

Schools and the Transmission of the Modern/Industrial Worldview

The dissemination of the modern/industrial worldview did not occur automatically. This process has been facilitated by the spread of cultural, economic, and political institutions that necessitated a qualitative break with the rural and agricultural worldview and social relations that existed prior to the industrial and urban revolutions. Schooling has been one of the primary vehicles through which succeeding generations have been inducted into the behavioral patterns and expectations encountered in these new institutions (Bowles and Gintis, 1976; Carnoy and Levin, 1985; Dreeben, 1977; Hogan, 1982; Inkeles and Smith, 1974). Schools have also served as a vehicle for allocating the population of modern states into new occupational positions (Bowles and Gintis, 1976; Collins, 1979; Leacock, 1969; Meyer, 1977; Parsons, 1959; Spring, 1972) as well as for developing the intellectual and practical skills required for a continued expansion of the forces of production (Dale, 1982; Floud and Halsey, 1959; Schrag, 1986).

Schools have achieved these ends by supplanting the role family and neighbors once played in preparing the young for participation in adult society. Changes in socialization practices in fact were necessitated as the market became an increasingly dominant factor in economic life and more people were drawn into the impersonal forms of authority and conformity that it demanded. Given their parochial and insular nature, primary groups such as the family were no longer able to prepare the young effectively for social interactions they would encounter beyond the home and immediate neighborhood. Nor were they able to prepare children for the forms of economic activity that would await them in the industrial factories and offices that were becoming the dominant sites of production and employment. Some institution was needed to bridge the gap between primary groups and the broader society (Bender, 1978; Dreeben, 1968; Durkheim, 1925/1961).

In the United States, state-supported schools were developed in part to serve as the vehicle by which children could be brought into this new social and economic reality. Early in the 1800s social elites became concerned that a number of trends, some of which promised to increase their own wealth and power, were threatening social order and stability. The expansion of East Coast cities was increasing both the geographic and social distance between the rich and poor, attenuating relationships based upon deference and ascribed authority. The influx of large numbers of Catholic immigrants and the development of class-based urban ghettos had also reduced their influence over the less privileged (Church and Sedlak, 1976, 71–73). These elites, many of whom were associated with the Whig Party, also feared that urbanization and industrialization would erode the ability of traditional social institutions such as the family and church to enforce conformity with generally agreed-upon social mores. To replace these weakened sites of moral guidance, they proposed that the state compel children to attend publicly supported schools where they would receive the forms of instruction believed necessary to maintain civil order. Within the schools the merchant and professional class could "reach down into the lower portions of the population and teach children there to share the values, ideals, and controls held by the rest of society" (Church and Sedlak, 1976, 79).

Horace Mann, one of the most important of the Whig reformers, justified the creation of a state-sponsored educational system on the grounds that it would prevent dishonesty, fraud, violence, and civil disorder. He argued that such an institution should be supported with taxes for the same reason that the citizenry taxed itself to employ law enforcement officers (Mann, 1848, 103–104). For Mann, the common school must become the "mother" who would train children in the virtues of piety, justice, truth, patriotism, benevolence, sobriety, industry, frugality, chastity, moderation, and temperance (Mann, 1848, 106). Will Herberg (1961) argues that common schools were able to contribute to this end by usurping the role that religion once had played as an instrument of moral instruction and social unification. In the place of a multitude of different religious faiths and values, all contending with one another for right of place, the schools could transmit a moral system that drew upon common religious themes, yet transcend them by being associated with no specific sect.

Common school reformers also believed that it was important to prepare the young to participate in that society occupationally as well as socially. As members of the propertied class, they stood to gain from economic developments made possible by new industrial innovations, and sought means by which the growing population in the United States could be prepared to contribute its labor to this process. Mann opened his *Twelfth Annual Report* (1848) with this panegyric about the development of human resources:

> Under the Providence of God, our means of education are the grand machinery by which the "raw material" of human nature can be worked up into inventors and discoverers, into skilled artisans and scientific farmers, into scholars and jurists, into the founders of benevolent institutions, and the great expounders of ethical and theological science. By the means of early education, those embryos of talent may be quickened...(79)

Mann believed that through education the poor would acquire the knowledge and skills required to lift themselves out of poverty, not by collectively challenging the already-privileged, but through individual initiative and effort. With proper training they could gain access to the wealth that was waiting to be exploited on the North American continent (Mann, 1848, 89), thereby improving both their own condition and the condition of the broader society. Church and Sedlak (1976, 67) point out that although such claims are ubiquitous in the writings of the common school reformers, nowhere did they indicate exactly how education would result in increases in productivity and inventiveness. They simply assumed that the dissemination of "intelligence" would lead to these results.

Perhaps more important and more justifiable, however, was the Whig belief that schooling would improve the work habits of the populace. Early manufacturers noted that educated workers were more reliable and efficient. They were also more willing to accept the authority of their employers and to obey institutional regulations (Bowles and Gintis, 1976, 162–63). In a survey accompanying his *Fifth Annual Report*, Mann questioned factory owners and superintendents about the relationship between education and labor. They responded that educated employees were more orderly, kept their machinery in better condition, and displayed greater punctuality, industriousness, and frugality (Church and Sedlak, 1976, 69). Such employees were more attuned to the rhythms of factories, rather than the rhythms of nature, and more accepting of labor that required them to function as adjuncts to machines. With a dramatic shift away from agricultural to industrial employment in the mid-nineteenth century, the preparation of such workers became a significant social concern. In Massachusetts, for example, the percentage of the work force engaged in farming fell from 58 percent in 1820 to 15 percent by 1850 (Bowles and Gintis, 1976, 165). The economic as well as social developments of this era thus appeared to necessitate fundamental changes in the socialization of children.

Dewey (1916/1966, 93–95) notes this dynamic in observations about the creation of state-supported schools in Germany. Under Prussian rule in the nineteenth century, the educational system from elementary school through university was centralized and directed toward furnishing the nation with the personnel it needed to accomplish military and industrial ends. Schooling in Germany became a means by which the activities of individuals could be coordinated to serve the political and economic purposes of the state. This is one of the first instances in which political leaders took active steps to provide for their population the disciplinary training required for participation in modern institutions (Dewey, 1916/1966, 94). This development recalls Foucault's (1977) assertion that education has played a pivotal role in spreading the disciplinary power required for political and economic centralization in the aftermath of the revolutions of the seventeenth and eighteenth centuries.

Meyer (1980) argues that even in the United States, where public education has never fallen under the control of the national government, widespread agreement about the function of common schools has led them to become a primary means for increasing the susceptibility of children to centralized political and economic institutions. Schools have furthered this end by replacing sacred and primordial explanations about "the nature and organization of personnel and knowledge" with explanations more in keeping with the needs of modern society (66). Although this process has presented new possibilities for individuals, particularly in regard to claims for equality, it has also "redefine[d] individuals as responsible subordinate members (and agents) of the state organization, and open[ed] them to new avenues of control and manipulation" (70).

In disregarding and then diminishing the role institutions such as the home, community, and church once played in the socialization of children, schools have encouraged the dissemination of two critical principles of the modern/industrial worldview: individualism and centralization. They have replaced more localistic and sectarian forms of morality with a set of secular universal values constructed in such a way as to subsume all other traditions. In doing so, they have helped to realign the loyalty of individuals away from immediate human associations to the impersonal organizations that have come to dominate modern society. This realignment, however, has not led to the formation of the deeper human ties and alliances characteristic of the kin group or small community, but has instead contributed to the atomization of the body politic. As if in response to this atomization, schools have also served as the site where children are taught the behavioral patterns and discipline required to participate in large organizations.

In their attempt to explain the process of modernization, a number of contemporary sociologists have argued that schools have in fact played the role Whig reformers hoped they would in preparing children for the demands of contemporary society (Dreeben, 1968; Inkeles and Smith, 1974; Parsons, 1959). Robert Dreeben (1968), in particular, has suggested that it is within schools that children are exposed to norms which are critical to their successful negotiation of modern economic and political institutions. These norms include independence, achievement, universalism, and specificity, norms which Dreeben believes cannot be transmitted within the home or other intimate social environments because of their more communal and localistic orientation. Within the impersonal and formal environment of classrooms, however, children can learn the individualistic yet closely monitored social relations associated with a market society.

Independence, for Dreeben, means "being self-reliant, accepting personal responsibility for one's behavior, acting self-sufficiently, and handling tasks with which, *under different circumstances* [Dreeben's emphasis], one can rightfully expect the help of others" (66). The acceptance of this norm is essential when individuals are thought of as wage earners, accountable to their employer for independently fulfilling the tasks for which they are paid. As capitalism developed in the West, the collaborative behavior and collective responsibility encountered on family farms or in family businesses did not match the forms of assembly-line production that were coming to dominate industrial practices.

By *achievement*, Dreeben means "activity and mastery, making an impact on the environment rather than fatalistically accepting it, and competing against some standard of excellence" (70). Dreeben acknowledges that families as well as schools develop a concern about achievement; such a concern is also encountered in premodern societies. Within the context of most families and earlier societies, however, individual worth is not measured against some abstract and impersonal standard of excellence; instead, worth is simply ascribed to the individual as a result of his or her being a member of the group. As Dreeben indicates, in such settings "status and support are guaranteed even if [people] fail to contribute to the best of their ability" (129). In contrast, in a market society individuals must be prepared to perform to the best of their ability or risk the judgments of others regarding their value as paid workers, judgments that can adversely affect their ability to provide for their own economic well-being.

As norms, independence and achievement are expressions of the individualistic rather than collective orientation of members of a market society. The third and fourth norms identified by Dreeben, *universalism* and *specificity*, parallel the equally important modern phenomenon of centralization. Dreeben defines universalism as the proclivity to respond to others as members of categorical groups rather than to characteristics that make them unique (74–75). The concept of universalism was initially defined by Parsons, who paired it with its opposite, particularism. Within the context of families and small communities, people relate to one another as particular members of an in-group. Outside that context, interactions with strangers are based upon their possession of more generalizable traits. Dreeben suggests that the willingness to perceive others as members of categorical groups is pivotal to the principle of equity or fairness, since a failure to transcend the particularism of the in-group is likely to result in "nepotism, favoritism, and arbitrariness" (74). Universalism is thus tied to another primary rule of the marketplace, which insists that individuals set aside in-group loyalties and obligations to protect civil peace and to maintain unimpeded trade. Through their acceptance of the norm of universalism, individuals become more willing to tolerate the regulations developed by centralized institutions to govern the corporate life of strangers.

The norm of specificity

> refers to the scope of one person's interest in another; to the obligation to confine one's interest to a narrow range of characteristics and concerns, or to extend them to include a broad range. The notion of relevance is implicit; the characteristics and concerns that should be included within the range, whether broad or narrow, are those considered relevant in terms of the activities in which the persons in question are involved. (Dreeben, 1968, 75)

The acquisition of this norm is a necessity if individuals are to negotiate the variety of relationships that have become part of life in the
modern world. In societies prior to our own, relationships were limited to a narrower range of people with whom one interacted in a variety of capacities. Within this social milieu, as in the family, people
responded to one another in a more holistic manner. In our own society, the complex division of labor that has been one of the products of
modernization now requires us to deal with others not as whole people, but as the providers of specific services. Whereas we continue to
interact with family members and immediate friends as the possessors of diffuse rather than specific roles, increasingly more of our relationships with others are defined by the marketable services they can
offer to us. Our concern about them as whole people is similarly narrowed.

Dreeben's short list of norms provides a useful handle for
understanding the important role that schools have played in the process of modernization. It is through the acquisition of such norms that
children have been able to make the transition from the mutually supportive social relations of agricultural villages to the more instrumental relations of the market. Within the context of classrooms, children
learn to align themselves with broad social values and become willing
to play specific roles within the structure of the surrounding society.
They also develop the competence required to perform the roles that
they either choose or are informally assigned (Parsons, 1959, 294).
Though there is little agreement about the specific causal relationship
between public education and modernization, the location of first
causes seems less important than the recognition of the intimate tie
that exists between these phenomena.

It is important to note that schools have not been simply
imposed upon unwilling populations. Resistance to the creation of
state-supported common schools was widespread in the 1800s and
has been recurrent in one form or another throughout the history of
American education. Because of the relationship between the skills
and dispositions transmitted by the schools and the requirements of a
changing economic environment, however, many parents were quick
to understand the advantage that schooling would bring to their children as they sought to advance their own welfare in a competitive job
market. Members of the working class, therefore, increasingly
demanded public schools as means to improve their own lives
(Hogan, 1982; Reese, 1986). Although they were not insensitive to the
way in which the lessons of the common school diminished their children's loyalty to family and community traditions, the possibilities of

economic mobility predicated upon academic success outweighed these less material concerns.

In the remainder of this chapter, I explore in more detail the interrelationship that exists between elements of the modern/industrial worldview and the structures, processes, and content encountered in contemporary American schools. Though it was the hope of early common-school reformers and later proponents of state-supported education that schools could be utilized as vehicles for drawing children into broader forms of social and cultural membership, such membership has not arisen in the way they had hoped. Instead, in conjunction with economic and political institutions, schools have contributed to a reduction in the amount of time families and members of human associations such as neighborhoods and churches can spend with one another (Bronfenbrenner, 1986; Coleman and Hoffer, 1987). They have also reduced children's need to acquire knowledge and social practices important for their own welfare from parents and neighbors (Ignatieff, 1984; McKnight, 1984). In subtle ways, the schools have contributed to the social disintegration they were set up to reverse. Of central concern in what follows is the way in which mass education has furthered, through its transmission of the modern/industrial worldview and the social relations characteristic of it, the forms of detachment discussed in Chapter 2. It is this detachment from surrounding social and natural environments that now seems so problematic.

Making Modern Citizens

Schools induct children into the modern world not so much by exposing them to a particular intellectual curriculum as through habituating them to forms of social organization and behavior characteristic of contemporary institutions. As Philip Jackson (1968) has noted, children spend approximately 1000 hours a year in classrooms. There they experience an environment that is remarkably stylized, stable, and repetitious, an environment in which "the physical objects, social relations, and major activities remain much the same from day to day, week to week, and even, in certain respects, from year to year" (9). These ongoing patterns become second nature, part of the definition of common sense and reality from which children construct their image of the world. Jackson further indicates that children soon learn that it is the maintenance of these institutional patterns, what he and others have called the hidden curriculum, which often seems to be the most important lesson taught by the school.

...every school child quickly learns what makes teachers angry. He learns that in most classrooms the behavior that triggers the teacher's ire has little to do with wrong answers or other indicators of scholastic failure. Rather it is violations of institutional expectations that really get under the teacher's skin. Typically, when a student is scolded by the teacher it is not because he has failed to spell a word correctly or to grasp the intricacies of long division. He is scolded, more than likely, for coming into the room late, or for making too much noise, or for not listening to directions, or for pushing while in line. (22)

In his essays on moral education, Durkheim also (1925/1961) observes that it is the internalization of these patterns of behavior that constitutes one of the most powerful lessons of the school.

If teachers and parents were more consistently aware that nothing can happen in the child's presence which does not leave some trace in him, that the form of his mind and of his character depends on these thousands of little unconscious influences that take place at every moment and to which we pay no attention because of their apparent insignificance, how much more would they watch their language and their behavior.... when education is patient and continuous, when it does not look for immediate and obvious successes, but proceeds slowly in a well-defined direction, without letting itself be diverted by external incidents and adventitious circumstances, it has at its disposal all the means necessary to affect minds profoundly. (86)

Part of the power of the school arises simply from the fact that when children are in classrooms they are not with primary group members, nor are they interacting with the natural world in an immediate and direct manner. They are thus denied the experience of socialization they would once have encountered in these environments prior to the creation of the school. It is now generally agreed that the "immersion into structured forms of social practice" (Hogan, 1982) encountered in schools provides an important means by which children are prepared for the exigencies of modern life. Before going on to an exploration of the ways that different school structures and practices contribute to the adoption of the modern/industrial worldview, it is useful to consider what children *not* in school once encountered in the process of growing up.

Cultural Transmission in Premodern Societies

Prior to the invention of the common school, most children learned about the natural and social worlds around them through their own investigations, through observing and imitating older children and adults, through play, through listening to stories, and through forms of instruction that were linked to the performance of necessary tasks. Although some learning occurred in the kinds of formal settings we associate with modern schools—especially learning related to the mastery of religious lore or texts—most children learned by actively participating in the life of their society (Spindler, 1974). Predicated on involvement, such learning encourages an engaged rather than detached orientation to the world. The knowledge children possess is grounded in experience and interaction. It is essentially concrete, rather than abstract. In other words, in such situations much of the knowledge children possess is their own, born from their dealings with the natural and social worlds that surround them.

Eskimo children, for example, are encouraged to explore local surroundings and participate in the activities of adults from early childhood on. Even very young children are given chores and are made to feel important for contributing to the family's well-being. At the same age that American children begin their long and segregated preparation for adulthood, Eskimo children begin to learn the skills they will use as adults in settings where their efforts have immediate and concrete effect. Learning for these children is not abstract and removed from the life of their communities; it is instead embedded within that community and the natural environment of which it is a part.

Although not burdened with responsibility, both boys and girls are expected to take an active role in family chores. In the early years responsibilites are shared, depending on who is available. Regardless of sex, it is important for a child to know how to perform a wide variety of tasks and give help when needed. Both sexes collect and chop wood, get water, help carry meat and other supplies, oversee younger siblings, run errands for adults, feed the dogs, and burn trash.

As a child becomes older, more specific responsibilities are allocated to him, according to his sex. Boys as young as seven may be given an opportunity to shoot a .22 rifle, and at least a few boys in every village have killed their first caribou by the time they are ten. A youngster learns techniques of butchering while on hunting trips with older siblings and adults, although he is seldom proficient until he is in his mid-teens. In the past girls learned butchering at an early age, since this knowledge was essential to attracting a good husband (Chance, 1966 25-26).

As George Spindler observes about this process: "Children are participants in the flow of life. They learn by observing and doing" (1974, 294). In our own society, such learning has become increasingly remote as children have been compelled to spend a major share of their childhood in buildings where immediate contact with nature and adults other than their teachers is denied to them.

Even though contemporary Amish children do in fact attend school, their parents have taken pains to assure that their offspring achieve enough contact with the work of adults and the requirements of farm life to guarantee the transmission of fundamental elements of their own tradition. These elements cannot be transmitted through the pages of books and the isolation of classrooms, but are instead shared, like the tasks learned in an Eskimo village, through learning that comes from direct rather than mediated involvement. This is particularly true when Amish children have reached puberty and are old enough to assume major homemaking or farming responsibilities. The Amish have insisted that public school officials allow them to run their own apprenticeship programs so that their children "can help along with the necessary work, and thereby learn their life vocation by doing" (Hostetler and Huntington, 1971, 75). The journal of one 14-year-old boy

> describes fixing various engines and machines that break down; digging up and cleaning piping; rebuilding a kitchen; rebuilding the chicken house; cementing and building a cow pen; butchering; plowing, disking, harrowing, and rolling the various fields; cleaning the barn; hauling manure; helping with the washing; and innumerable other tasks essential to farm management. (Hostetler and Huntington, 1971, 75)

Through such learning experiences, children come to know their place both in their family and on the land. They come to know the world as something not separate from themselves but as closely related to their own identities and obligations, something the Amish believe is essential if their children are to become fully participating members of their communities.

Although it is important to observe that much of the learning experienced by either Eskimo or Amish children would be insufficient preparation for life in industrialized societies, the way adults in these cultures have integrated teaching and learning into the texture of their day-to-day life remains instructive. Learning occurs within a social context where effort is tied to the completion of tasks valued by the community. Children learn not for themselves alone, but for others. Furthermore, they do so in ways that demonstrate to them the importance of their mastery of knowledge and skills that make it possible to interact with the surrounding environment in an efficacious and sustainable manner. Embedded within social and natural communities, they are reminded continually of their relatedness and interdependence. It is this relatedness and interdependence that children's experience in contemporary schools erodes and weakens. Of central concern here is how this has happened.

Detaching Children from Adults

One of the most important lessons children learn in classrooms is to develop relations with adults and peers that are qualitatively different from those they will have experienced within most noninstitutional settings prior to the beginning of elementary school. In school, children are expected to become significantly more independent of adult attention and aid than they are at home.[1] This relationship is in part linked to organizational structures predicated on the fact that schools are populated with large numbers of children and small numbers of educators (Jackson, 1968). In most classrooms of 25 to 30 students, teachers simply cannot give each child the same kind of time and attention that his or her adult caregivers in smaller social settings can provide. In classrooms, children must acquire the ability to complete tasks on their own. They learn from their teachers that the forms of mutual support most will have experienced at home are not encountered in the same way in the broader society.

This emphasis on independence can affect not only a child's relationship with adults in school, but also his or her relation with adults at home. This is particularly true in regard to work upon which a child's abilities are evaluated. Although parental assistance in the early grades is often encouraged, as children become older and measures of individual ability become more significant, the school comes to frown upon forms of family support that children might otherwise take for granted. This practice, however, teaches children that not only their teachers but also their parents cannot be relied upon to help them in one of the primary environments in which their self-worth is measured and defined, forcing them to develop a measure of detached independence they would be unlikely to learn at home.

Also contributing to the development of detached relations with adults is the fact that within most schools children are exposed to serial rather than long-term relationships with teachers. During elementary school, students will encounter a number of teachers who could potentially become as significant as other adults they have come to love and depend upon. One of the early arguments for employing women as elementary school teachers was based on the premise that children would more easily respond to a person who resembled their principal caregivers at home. In contrast to family relationships, however, the relationships formed in school are systematically broken on a regular basis. This pattern of forming and breaking relationships increases in frequency as children move into secondary school, where they will face a larger number of teachers. In many respects, the transient relations with adults that children encounter in school prepare them for the transient relations they are likely to establish with most people in the broader society throughout the remainder of their lives. It could be argued that such relations may also prepare students to see ties to even their own parents as temporary, making it easier for them to move away from family or community obligations in the same way they have been taught to move away from their teachers.

Not only are the relations between students and teachers in school impermanent, they are predominantly characterized by emotional coolness. As the crowding encountered in many schools precludes the offering of support to most students, it also generally precludes the formation of meaningful, if only short-lived, emotional attachments. But the absence of such bonding is not simply a matter of school structure. As Dreeben (1968, 30) observes, teachers are customarily expected to avoid intense expressions of either verbal or physical affection. They are to remain congenial but distanced from their students, establishing relationships more characteristic of commercial transactions than friendship, relationships which look much more like the relations established between employers and employees than those encountered within primary groups (Jackson, 1968, 31). In this way, children are prepared to enter a market society where dealings with others are governed not by forms of emotional attachment, obligation, and loyalty, but by the observance of externally determined rules of behavior.

Part of the detached superficiality characteristic of student-teacher relationships is also linked to the fact that school teachers as well as students are given well-defined and limited roles. Children learn that most teachers respond only to certain kinds of requests and circumscribe their relationships with the majority of students to a narrow range of tasks and interactions. Coping with this environment helps children learn to limit their expectations of others and seek them out for the specific services they can provide.

Children learn that their roles, as well, are restricted. Only certain forms of behavior are appropriate within classrooms. The tears or anger or enthusiasm that are a natural part of their lives at home are proscribed in school. School becomes emotionally flat and increasingly devoid of the personal (Goodlad, 1984, 242–43). As Dreeben notes, the shallow and fleeting relationships based upon these roles increases "the likelihood that pupils will have experiences in which the fullness of their individuality is *not* involved, as it tends to be in their relationships among kin and close friends" (1968, 79).

Finally, as Eisenstadt (1956) has noted, schools have weakened ties between children and adults by focusing on the transmission of instrumental knowledge rather than cultural values and meanings, a task theoretically left to families and churches. This has meant that children are no longer receiving, at least within the school, sustained instruction in the forms of social practice essential to the maintenance of interdependent communities. Bernstein (1975) has suggested that in the absence of sustained exposure to cultural rituals and values, students must turn to one another to achieve their own sense of validation and personal meaning. He asserts that the rise of adolescent gangs and youth culture is linked to the failure of adults to draw children into values that contribute to the experience of social membership rather than isolation.

Detaching Students from One Another

Not only do schools teach children to relate with adults in a much more circumscribed way, they also tend to inhibit the ability of children to transfer the forms of supportive relationships generally encountered among primary groups to one another. This does not mean that children fail to form new bonds with their peers; obviously, many children do make friends and establish supportive networks that to some extent replicate the social relations found among family members and neighbors (Cusick, 1973). Rather than encouraging the formation of such groups, however, the organizational regularities encountered within schools have generally been aimed at preventing such ties from becoming a dominant factor in the lives of students, inhibiting the ability of many children to experience a sense of membership within the broader school community (Gregory and Smith, 1987). Extracted from their home environments and prevented from developing supportive bonds with their teachers, students are given few opportunities to create legitimate associations within which they might learn the skills and dispositions required to act collectively as members of a common institution. Instead, they are led to turn their attention to their own self-interest or the interest of small groups while ignoring the interests of the entire school.

This weaning of children from the forms of affiliation and support encountered within families and well-functioning communities is furthered by the way in which students are scheduled into the school's activities. In junior and senior high schools, in particular, students attend classes with an ever-changing array of peers, many of whom will be strangers unless the student is tracked into a small group of either high or low achievers. Interviews conducted during a study of programs for at-risk youth raised this issue in a particularly poignant way (Wehlage, Rutter, Smith, Lesko, and Fernandez, 1989). When the scheduling process separates students from a handful of friends, they may spend their entire day in the company of strangers. In response, some students cut classes in order to relieve the experience of loneliness and isolation they encounter within the school.

Scheduling is complemented by forms of instructional practice that also tend to inhibit social interaction and teach children to be alone in a crowd. Unlike most social environments children will have encountered prior to school, in classrooms they must learn to ignore those around them for long periods of time. As Jackson (1968) reports:

> In elementary classrooms students are frequently assigned seatwork on which they are expected to focus their individual energies. During these seatwork periods talking and other forms of communication between students are discouraged, if not openly forbidden. The general admonition in such situations is to do your own work and leave others alone. In a sense, then, students must try to behave as if they were in solitude, when in point of fact they are not. They must keep their eyes on their paper when human faces beckon. (16)

Although students find ways to subvert this common expectation, schools remain places where personal interaction is discouraged and often punished. Students who cannot learn to be "alone in a crowd" are generally considered to be behavior problems. Over time, if they are unable or unwilling to adjust to this requirement, many will find themselves increasingly cut off from the school's rewards.

Most conventional evaluation procedures also inhibit the formation of student groups by setting students against one another in a

competition for grades. These procedures act to discourage cooperation. Johnson and Johnson (1974) have noted, for example, that when
students are graded in comparison with others, they hurt themselves
when they help their peers. This dynamic can lead to increased hostili-
ty and mutual distrust among students (228), as well as increased student isolation from one another (225). In their study of an urban middle school, Schofield and Sagar found that although such competition
was strongest among successful students, it was apparent throughout
the entire school population (1979, 174). Herndon (1965) and Schwartz
(1981), furthermore, have noted the role of competition as a divisive
factor in social relations among underachieving students. Such students tend to differentiate themselves from their peers, disparaging
the work of those who make academic efforts and yet accusing one
another of being stupid or cheating. To maintain their own self-
esteem, such students seek to shake off in whatever way they can the
school's judgment that they are inadequate. The school's evaluative
procedures thus further inhibit the establishment of solidarity among
those students teachers often fear most.

On the occasions when teachers attempt to encourage more
cooperation, students trained in the dominant style of the school may
see such efforts as an impediment to their own academic achievement.
Deutsch (1962, 283) has found that students concerned about advancing their own position cannot allow themselves to be deflected by the
academic needs or demands of their peers. Cooperation for such students threatens to diminish their own chances for success. More
recently, Schofield and Sagar (1979) discovered a similar dynamic in
the resistance of students to cooperative learning activities if they perceived that such projects threatened their individual academic
progress. They recount an incident in a classroom where group projects had been assigned. A high-achieving boy objected to his placement in a group consisting of what he perceived to be less able students. Despite orders from his teacher to accept his membership in this
group, he initially attempted to work on his own and then resorted to
forming his own group. At the end of the class, he said to the teacher,
"I come here for my own education, not for somebody else's" (1979,
163). In the atomized social settings encountered in most classrooms,
this highly individualistic viewpoint is not uncommon and serves to
diminish the importance of broader student associations.

Detaching Children from Local and Personal Knowledge

Schools not only contribute to the development of social relations characterized by independence and detachment, they also

diminish the importance of forms of knowledge and traditions associated with primary groups or personal experience. The knowledge conveyed in school is the knowledge of people who have accepted the tenets of the modern/industrial worldview. Knowledge that is more regional in nature, tied into nonindustrial economic practices, or premised on nonscientific approaches to natural phenomena is given little credence.

Willard Waller (1932/1967) was one of the first observers to note that teachers represent a wider cultural variant that often stands in opposition to the culture of many public school students and their families. As indicated earlier, the knowledge and social practices transmitted by educators represent the knowledge and social practices deemed valuable not by entire communities but by members of certain classes within those communities, especially members of the middle class who align themselves with the values of the marketplace and forms of knowledge predicated on objectivity and rationalism. This conflict between what might be termed the culture of the center and the culture of the periphery was more evident throughout the entire population earlier in this century. Then, some children in white ethnic, rural, and working-class groups resisted the bourgeois culture that was becoming increasingly significant as the nation became urbanized and industrialized. As a growing share of the white population has been drawn into the middle class during the twentieth century, however, this conflict has become one between a dominant bourgeois culture and the cultures of racial and non-European ethnic minorities. Throughout the history of the common school mastering the school's culture has often led children to reject the primary groups from which they came (Fordham, 1988; Gans, 1962; Rodriguez, 1982; Steinetz and Solomon, 1986; Weis, 1985).

In addition to detaching children from the knowledge transmitted by their own social groups, schools also diminish the importance of the knowledge they construct out of their own experience in the world. Nearly all school instruction occurs in classrooms cut off from the natural environment. Within four walls, the world is generally studied at a distance, from books or behind glass, or from the images of films and videotapes. The contact with the earth, animals, plants, and weather that would have been the stuff of the education of children in pre-modern societies is mediated in contemporary schools (Shepard, 1982). With the exception of the rare field trip, children only go outside to play. We teach them, by inference, that real learning happens inside and is composed of something other than their own natural observations. Although schools cannot be held solely responsible for this form of alienation, they are accomplices in the process of detachment from a lived interaction with nature that begins in most contemporary homes and will continue into the workplace.

Within the classroom, the process by which children learn about that world serves to remove them further from any meaningful form of contact with it. Rather than encouraging a sense of participation with and wonder about the natural environment, most school instruction treats the world as something that is abstract and other. Students are given few opportunities to explore the world in ways that might lead to a deeper sense of identification with the environment. They are instead taught commonly accepted explanations and learn to treat the world as an objective and mechanical reality. Reflecting on her own experience as a student, educator Eleanor Duckworth (1991) laments that throughout her years in school she was only twice "given the opportunity to come up with my own ideas, a fact I consider typical and terrible" (1). Too few teachers attempt to make learning personal or to involve the learner himself or herself in the exploration and creation of new knowledge. Even a subject area like social studies becomes stripped of any deeper attention to human concerns and is reduced to little more than facts and places that must be memorized for tests (Goodlad, 1984, 212). In this situation, children are taught that the knowledge valued by their teachers is fundamentally different from that derived from their own relationship with the world, a relationship that is seen to possess little importance within the context of most classrooms (Esland, 1971, 84). Subjective participation is replaced by the accumulation of data that often is neither personal nor meaningful, only required.

Mary Metz (1978) has called this kind of instruction *incorporative education.* Teachers who approach their work from this perspective tend to think of knowledge

> as having a definite existence of its own. It is a tangible "body" of knowledge which must be "funneled into" the students. Interaction of the knowledge and the student in this process is not mentioned; the student simply incorporates the well-defined entity just as one's library shelf might receive a new book which is then "part" of the library. So this knowledge is now assumed to be part of the child, and he is ready for the next connected bit of knowledge in the next grade. (37)

Studies that have involved widespread observations in diverse schools tend to indicate that the incorporative approach to teaching and learning is frequently encountered (Goodlad, 1984). Within a classroom where this approach is utilized, children are expected to listen or read and then master and replicate the information presented by their teachers with little opportunity to share their own knowledge or ask their own questions.

Jackson (1968) has noted that structural features of most schools almost guarantee that children will be treated in this manner. When 20 to 30 people, if not more, are asked to live and work within the small space of a classroom, they must learn to limit their activities. Not doing so is likely to lead to conditions of disorder. The result, however, is that although the gestures of teaching and learning may go on in most classrooms, a significant proportion of children become mentally disengaged from the educational process. Over time, children respond to the delays, denial of desire, interruptions, and isolation inherent in this situation by becoming increasingly uninvolved. In a recent study, Sedlak et al. (1986) estimate that approximately two-thirds of American public school students are generally disengaged from the activities of their classrooms, indicating that such detachment may be part and parcel of the experience of formal schooling as it has evolved in the United States and elsewhere. In a fundamental way, schools seem to separate knowledge from life, turning a majority of students into passive spectators of teaching activities who see little relationship between the events of their classrooms and the requirements of responsible participation in the broader community.

Finally, school not only teaches children to devalue their own knowledge of the world; it also teaches them to detach themselves from their own desires and interests. In the process schooling breaks the link between self and experience. Within most classrooms, children learn to divide their lives into self-chosen and teacher-chosen activities. Jackson observes that the former activities are thought of as play, and the latter as work (1968, 30–31). To survive in school, students must set aside what they would like to do and do what they are told. To succeed in school, children must also set aside what they might like to think. As Jackson (1968) observes:

> At the heart of the teacher's authority is his command over the student's attention. Students are expected to attend to certain matters while they are in the classroom, and much of the teacher's energies are spent in making sure that this happens. At home the child must learn how to stop; at school he must learn how to look and listen. (30)

Children are thus led to adopt an instrumental attitude toward their own experience. While they view schooling as a source of neither pleasure nor joy, most students see classroom learning as necessary for the achievement of some future end. They tolerate it because they are conscious of the way it may help them later in life (Jackson, 1968, 48). In the process they learn the alienation from self that Marx observed is one of the fundamental characteristics of workers employed in wage labor.

Learning to Submit to Impersonal Authority

Many of the organizational and social characteristics of the school are predicated on the need to maintain order and control. The practices learned in school in fact prepare children for the conformity and compliance that will be required of them in most bureaucratic and centralized institutions. Durkheim, for example, suggests that an educational structure that precludes the formation of close interpersonal ties between teachers and students is in fact necessary if the school is to perform its task of inducting children into the social relations characteristic of modern society. As the school frees children from what Durkheim considers to be excessive dependency on the family, so must the school free them from excessive dependency upon individual teachers. Only in this way will the influence of the school become universal rather than particular, and the "abstract and impersonal rule" that should command human deference be linked to social institutions rather than the individuals who occupy positions within them (Durkheim, 1925/1961, 144–45). By being exposed to a variety of adults whose authority is tied not to personal characteristics but to their role within bureaucratic structures, Durkheim believes that children will come to associate that authority with society, the ultimate reference point for their moral decisions and actions.

The development of limited and clearly defined relations may be a necessary component of bureaucratic as opposed to communal organizations. Because the school does not generally allow children to develop the forms of interpersonal ties and commitments upon which authority in families and other primary groups is based, alternative steps must be taken to define new forms of authority based not upon affection but institutional position. Although differences in power also exist between a child and his or her parents, that relationship is characterized by intimacy and duration. Furthermore, as Jackson (1968) notes, a parent's authority, particularly during the preschool years, tends to be primarily restrictive, aimed at preventing the child from engaging in actions that might be dangerous or destructive. In contrast, the teacher's authority is both presciptive and restrictive. The teacher tells the child what to do as much as he or she tells the child what not to do. In many respects, the teacher functions as the child's first "boss," and in learning or not learning the work habits desired by this authoritative but impersonal adult, children develop patterns that will influence their performance in institutional settings throughout the remainder of their lives.

School strategies aimed at atomizing student populations also serve to sustain the power of those given authority in bureaucratic institutions. Waller (1932) argues that maintaining such divisions is in fact essential to the school because it is with students that the ultimate power in most educational institutions rests.[2] Because of their numbers, if students decide to resist the demands of their teachers, there will be little that their teachers can do to control them.

The school's imposition of its own grouping practices furthers the breakdown of the social relations students may bring with them to school and contributes to their induction into practices characteristic of highly centralized societies. First graders learn, for example, that their most important distinguishing characteristics are their age and ability to read, not the fact that they are members of a particular family, come from a particular neighborhood, or attend a particular church. This process theoretically diminishes the importance of unique and potentially divisive characteristics related to family background and circumstance. As Dreeben notes,

> within the classroom, all pupils very close in age and in capacities related to age, occupy a single position, are given similar work assignments, confront the same teacher, and are treated very much alike in instructional and disciplinary matters. Stated differently, under these conditions, much more than in the family, pupils have an opportunity to view each other and themselves as sharing common experiences, and as being in the same boat despite the obvious personal differences among them. (1968, 22)

Though schools are only partially successful in reducing the importance of individual differences, "the process of sequential categorization ...provides settings in which individuals form an increasing number of new equalities, and thereby provides situations in which [students] can learn how to subordinate differences to similarities, both specifically and generally" (Dreeben, 1968, 109).

Finally, the school's evaluation procedures serve to elicit student allegiance to the goals and values of the school in opposition to the goals and values of the peer group. In this regard, Esland (1971, 84) has noted that evaluation is the means by which a student's compliance with the epistemology of the school is measured. Grades are both sanctions and rewards upon which children construct their image of themselves. Through ongoing evaluation, schools extract individuals from the groups to which they had previously belonged, rewarding those who possess the attributes deemed valuable by the broader society (Schrag, 1986) and disregarding the psychological need for acceptance by students whose talents and skills may lie in other areas (Gardner, 1983). In this way children are prepared to accept the judgments of bureaucratic authorities about their personal merits, something which is in fact necessary if the differential rewards of the market are to be accepted by its participants.

Ethnographic studies of life in classrooms have tended to confirm the degree to which schools are able to impart critical lessons about life in centralized bureaucracies to children. Harry Gracey's (1972) study of kindergarten is illustrative of this research. He found that after being persistently drilled over the course of a year in a series of institutional routines, children came to respond to their teacher's commands with unquestioning and automatic compliance; they had become habituated to the school environment. Describing this process, Gracey writes:

> The social structure Edith [the teacher] has created in this room is a formidable molder of children's behavior and attitudes. She has established a complete set of routines and rituals for controlling the behavior of most children for most of the time they are in the room. The children, by the end of the year, have learned the elaborate rules and procedures, so that they move through the day automatically, in response to Edith's signals, from one routine to another, such as from work time to cleanup time. The children are occasionally allowed to choose within this framework, as between one song and another or between drawing and painting. There is, however, no room in this classroom organization for introducing any material from the spontaneous interests of the children. They are organized into a completely teacher-dominated group in which there is no provision for them to make significant contributions to the day's activities. (174)

Leacock (1969), Apple (1979), and Gearing and Epstein (1982), also point to the impact that social practices and school structures can have on children's behavior and development. Although not all children will abide by the school's institutional lessons to the same degree, those who do will be more likely to find acceptance by institutional authorities who make decisions about economic advancement and security.

Schooling and the Promise of Individual Advancement

When reduced to the level of the individual, the ideology of progress becomes the promise of social and economic mobility. The quest for a more materially comfortable and secure life has been at the heart of the American experiment (Gans, 1988). The dream of affluence continues to draw immigrants to the United States. It is also held out as one of the primary reasons for enduring the lessons of the school. In the 1950s and 1960s, differences in the earnings of high-school and college graduates were printed on disposable textbook covers, reminding students daily of the economic benefits of postsecondary education. In the 1980s and 1990s, posters proclaiming that school dropouts will earn half a million dollars less than their colleagues who graduate can be found in the offices of middle- and high-school counselors. The possibilities of betterment, however, are universally portrayed in individualistic terms. It is through the achievement of individual students that progress will be gained, not through collective effort. In fact, students who continue to seek their security through patterns of mutual support encountered in well-functioning primary groups often find themselves at odds with the school. In a fundamental way, the ideology of progress provides the rationale for relinquishing all that must be sacrificed to succeed both in school and in a market society.

For children in the middle class, these sacrifices are generally unquestioned. The social construction of maturity involves leaving family and home communities for college and work. Without the willingness of people to accept this kind of geographic mobility, many contemporary institutions would find it difficult to locate and cultivate the "human capital" they need to function. For children from working-class, ethnic, or economically disadvantaged backgrounds, however, such mobility threatens to disrupt patterns of relationship that, if abandoned, can seriously affect personal well-being and security. Although the communal structures encountered in such settings can lead to the perpetuation of poverty, they also provide what may be one of the few means of support in highly unpredictable economic and social environments (Connell, Ashenden, Kessler, Dowsett, 1982; Stack, 1975; Steinetz and Solomon, 1986).

In her study of black students in an urban community college, Weis (1985) points out the degree to which attempting to achieve academic success can jeopardize this kind of support. Although many of the students she studied wished to attain success in the dominant economy, doing so often meant cutting ties with extended family members and neighbors in order to make the leap into the middle class. That leap entailed adopting the cultural categories and behaviors desired by teachers who represent mainstream society. These behaviors, such as punctuality and good attendance, counter social responsibilities and obligations to others in a social network predicated on cooperation and mutual aid.

In the community college that was the focus of Weis's research, black students who succeeded were those willing to become like their professors, most of whom were white and middle class. Black professors at the college were even more resolutely middle class than their white colleagues. To the two or three students in each course willing to adopt their cultural perspective and the behaviors associated with it, professors devoted their attention and care. With other students, unusually strict attendance or evaluation policies resulted in their being dropped from classes or failed. In this situation, progress or economic mobility rested on the willingness of students to define themselves as individuals apart from the collective social environment they had known since childhood.

Borman et al. (1988) consider a similar phenomenon among urban Appalachian girls and young women. They observe that

> Since the function of schooling in American society is ostensibly to provide an avenue of mobility for those who learn the "proper" attitudes and skills reflected in the schools' predominantly middle-class standards, Appalachian youth who are reluctant to give up their own cultural heritage will remain alienated. Even if they see advantage in acquiring school-related standards for success, by the time they reach secondary school the processes of testing, labeling, sorting, and placement are likely to aim them toward academic careers set up for failure. (241)

Female students who in fact succeed in school are generally those who have cut interpersonal ties to their own community. They pursue friendships outside their neighborhoods and come to define themselves by other cultural values. In her study of successful black students in an urban high school, Fordham (1988) found students similarly adopting the cultural interests and values of the dominant society. This frequently led their black peers to charge them with "acting white." School people, themselves, often have little patience for students whose loyalty to family and friends supersedes their sense of obligation to their own education. As a counselor interviewed during Fine and Zane's (1988) study of low-income female dropouts remarked about a girl who had dropped out to care for her grandmother: "...if Portia is concerned about her future she needs not to get so involved in her family but worry about herself" (34).

Richard Rodriguez's (1982) account of the impact of his education on the experience of intimacy with his own family points out the costs of realigning loyalties away from primary groups to the possibility of individual progress. Although he and his siblings were pushed by their Latino parents to succeed in schools and master English as a means to advance themselves, their success in this endeavor drew them further and further away from the sense of closeness encountered in other Mexican-American families. Rodriguez himself says that in the process of succeeding in school he abandoned his parents as models of the person he wished to become and took on instead the persona of his teachers. As a child he would smile when his teachers noted that his parents must be proud of him; within, he knew how little pride he felt in them. In this way, the bonds between nonmiddle-class and/or minority children who succeed in school and their families and communities are attenuated. Having left that relationship, what remains is loneliness and the "hunger of memory." What's left as well is the need to succeed in a market society on its terms.

Schools serve as the arena in which the ideology of progress is first played out. While it is true that many children either resist the contest or decide to withdraw, the simple fact of their participation often results in their internalization of the school's judgment about their value and potential status (Sennett and Cobb, 1972). In the past, one's level of material well-being was largely given as a result of birth. In the United States especially, but other industrialized nations as well (Rohlen, 1983), that well-being is now assumed not to be a product of class background but of individual merit and motivation. In a market society, the poor are consigned to poverty because they do not possess the qualities deemed valuable by impersonal and inescapable economic forces. Correcting this situation is the responsibility of individuals who must strive to acquire the skills, dispositions, and manners required to present themselves as desirable commodities in a competitive labor market. Especially when education is universally available and free, those who do not take the steps necessary to escape their condition increasingly come to be seen as guilty of

their own impoverishment, a situation that will only be corrected
when and if they decide to participate in the demands of the school
and the broader economic institutions which it serves (Finn, 1987).

Conclusion

In a variety of ways, then, schools have acted to consolidate and
extend among their students a number of fundamental principles of
the modern/industrial worldview. By removing children from their
homes, neighborhoods, and the surrounding nonhuman physical
environment, schools have often led children to become increasingly
detached from their own experience of the world. Once they have
been brought into the school, educators have then inducted students
into social relations characterized primarily by the absence of sustained support or commitment. Children learn within the school that
they are individuals, cut off from their teachers and most of their
peers. Schools have also substituted new forms of centralized order
and control to regulate the lives of children released from obligations
and forms of authority found in families and traditional communities.
The maintenance of this order has led to the development of social
practices within schools that prevent the formation of informal associations among students, often setting them against one another in a
competition for the school's rewards. The incentive for accepting
these forms of detachment has been the promise of both economic
mobility and social progress tied to the development of alternative
forms of personal security, dependent not upon interpersonal commitments but individual effort.

Before leaving this chapter, however, it is important to note two
caveats. The first is that the school is by no means the only institution
responsible for inducting children into the modern/industrial worldview. Over the past three decades, for example, television has
assumed an increasingly important role in the socialization of the
young (Mander, 1978). It is largely from the TV that children are
exposed to what it means to be a successful (or unsuccessful) adult in
our society. It is there as well that they encounter an unending portrayal of the promised land of material wealth and comfort held out
by modern industrialism. As important as its content is the nature of
the medium of television, itself. Viewing TV is essentially a detached
and asocial activity. Children learn to experience their lives through
screens that mediate reality and turn it into collections of manageable
and impersonal images (Kubey and Csikszentmihalyi, 1990). Further-

more, they learn to be in the presence of human conversation without any possibility of interaction. The time children, as well as adults, spend sitting as silent observers in front of the television simply extends the lessons of nonparticipation and passivity they learn in school (or perhaps vice versa). This element of our common culture must also be addressed if we hope to move beyond the limitations of the modern/industrial worldview.

Second, it is critical to recognize that the lessons of the school have not been uncontested. As suggested at different points during the preceding discussion, people whose well-being has been predicated on premodern forms of knowledge or social practice have often resisted the lessons of the public school. Catholics, for example, were among the first groups to defy the plans of the common school reformers by creating their own separate educational system, aimed not at inducting their children into the secular and individualistic values set out by public schools, but at maintaining the integrity of their own communities and faith (Katz, 1971). Fundamentalist Christian congregations persist in such opposition today (Peshkin, 1986).

Similarly, rural families, although supporting their own public school systems, have tended to do so in ways that have not confirmed the emphasis on individual achievement and independence, universalism or specificity encountered in schools governed by members of the urban middle class. At least until widespread efforts to consolidate small schools, most children in rural areas were educated in classrooms that often affirmed rather than denied their membership in cohesive communities (Peshkin, 1977).

Finally, many children and parents from poor and working-class families have frequently seen little reason to adjust completely to the institutional requirements of the school, nor have they been given much sustained encouragement or support to do so. When the slim chance of translating academic success into economic success has been combined with the discordant relationship between the middle-class orientation of most teachers and their own family backgrounds and values, many economically disadvantaged students have found little reason to conform completely to the expectations of the school (Connell et al., 1982; Davies, 1984; Everhart, 1983; Fordham and Ogbu, 1986; Matute-Bianchi, 1986; McDermott, 1974; McDermott and Gospodinoff, 1979; Ogbu, 1978; Willis, 1977).

Also contributing to the less than complete induction of all children into the norms of the modern world is the fact that teachers have tended to favor students whose behavior and assumptions have matched the expectations of the school. Students from non-middle-class backgrounds unwilling or unable to learn what teachers want to teach have often been disregarded or poorly treated. This has meant that although the ideal of the common school has been to bring students from diverse groups into the shared economic and political life of the nation, in actual practice the American educational system has generally made it easier for middle-class students to master its lessons than children from other socioeconomic groups (Anyon, 1981; Church and Sedlak, 1976; Leacock, 1969; Wilcox, 1982).

Despite parent and student resistance and the disinclination or inability of teachers to educate all students equally, however, the related expansion of the forces of production and the nation-state has steadily contributed to the extension of education to a growing proportion of the population. With modernization, the economy came to provide a multiplicity of new occupational opportunities, access to which has been predicated on the possession of educational credentials. Working-class students who in the past could have afforded to disregard the school's offerings have become increasingly willing to tolerate an educational process that in some ways may counter their own values and beliefs (Steinetz and Solomon, 1986; Weis, 1988). Furthermore, as many of those positions have come to require workers capable of performing more sophisticated cognitive tasks, economic and political leaders as well as working-class parents have placed pressure upon the schools to alter their programs in ways that would appeal to previously uninterested students (Kliebard, 1986; Reese, 1986). What is questionable now is whether the detached social relations and forms of knowledge propagated by most schools are appropriate for the experience children will face in the coming century when economic stasis or contraction, rather than expansion, may be the rule.

Four

❂

A Sustainable Worldview

It seems likely that if the economic developments that have characterized the modern era were to persist in an uninterrupted fashion, allowing increasing numbers of individuals to enter the middle class, the forms of socialization provided by public schools in the United States would continue to offer most children the training they need to obtain security as adults. The development of independence, an achievement ethic, the ability to deal with others as the possessors of specific rather than diffuse roles, and an orientation to universal rather than local categories and forms of membership would continue to facilitate a successful transition to the requirements of mainstream society. Although some populations could be expected to continue to resist this socialization, it seems plausible that the efficacy of conventional educational practice would gradually convince marginal populations able to join the mainstream to do so. With the exception of selected population groups in the United States, this pattern has been repeated for several decades (Ogbu, 1978). As indicated earlier, however, the continued expansion of occupational opportunities is now jeopardized by resource depletion and environmental deterioration. If this situation persists, schools will no longer be able to equip the majority of students with the skills or dispositions necessary to create their own security.

In an economy characterized by restricted rather than expanding opportunities and a need for greater sensitivity to the limitations of the natural world, a cultivation of detached independence from specific human and natural environments will no longer further the ability of children to care satisfactorily for themselves. In this situation, an educational format aimed at inducting children into the modern/industrial worldview will become inappropriate. For example, the belief that we stand apart from nature as objective observers and masters rather than one among a multiplicity of interrelated life forms could lead to a perpetuation of current economic practices that are now endangering the environment. The belief that individuals exist as social atoms, primarily responsible for their own well-being rather than the well-being of the broader community, could lead to the development of forms of competition and survivalism that would devastate public trust and order. The belief that centralization is the answer to fundamental problems related to economics and politics could preclude the evolution of local solutions to the problems we are likely to encounter if economic conditions worsen. Finally, the belief that the aim of human life is the attainment of higher and higher levels of material comfort and affluence could preclude the renaissance or development of ethical and religious systems capable of helping people to make a virtue out of a reduced standard of living and simpler lifestyle.

An educational process capable of helping children learn attitudes and forms of behavior more in keeping with significantly changed material conditions will have to be informed with a worldview whose fundamental assumptions lead not to the detachment characteristic of our own era but to forms of identification, participation, commitment, and accountability informed with a recognition of interdependence and interconnection with others. In the remainder of this chapter, I present a sketch of what the components of such a worldview may be and address what I see as central flaws of the modern/industrial worldview.

The discussion that follows, however, is not simply a result of my own analysis. On the margins of political life in nations around the globe a new environmentally oriented but as yet loosely structured social movement has been emerging in response to our current crisis. In some countries, this movement has coalesced into what has been called the Green Party. This movement has been constructed out of alliances among labor, Third World, peace, environmental, feminist, Christian, and community activists (Bahro, 1986; Boggs, 1986; Capra and Spretnak, 1984; Porritt, 1984). What distinguishes it from other contemporary political movements on the right and left is its preoccupation with ecological issues and the rejection of the ideology of unlimited material progress. Its members, more than any other political or social activists, are grappling with the economic, political, social, and cultural implications of the environmental crisis. Although a systematic presentation of the agendas associated with this movement would take us too far afield from the educational issues that are our focus here, my discussion of a sustainable worldview is closely tied to the thought of many of its participants.

The worldview that follows includes four primary assumptions drawn from the writings of environmental theoreticians and activists, as well as some of the critics of modernization whose insights contributed to the earlier discussion of the modern/industrial worldview (Bahro, 1986; Berman, 1981; Boggs, 1986; Bookchin, 1980; Bowers, 1987; Capra, 1983; Capra and Spretnak, 1984; Coates, 1981; D'Souza, 1989; Devall, 1980; Galtung, 1986; Green Party of Federal Republic of Germany, 1985; King, 1983, 1989; Merchant, 1980; Mewes, 1985; Oliver and Gershman, 1989; Ophuls, 1977; Sale, 1985, 1987, 1988; Salleh, 1984; Satin, 1987; Smith, 1982). These assumptions include the following:

1. Humankind is embedded in a physical universe that functions more as an organism than a machine. Rather than treating the universe as an *It*, we must treat it as a *Thou*, recognizing that we stand in a fundamental relationship to the natural environment from which we cannot extricate ourselves. The aim of knowledge is to further identification with that universe, rather than to master it.

2. The basic units of society are not isolated and possessive individuals but the primary groups or small communities in which they are embedded. Security and social health are achieved when individuals contribute to one another's well-being through cooperative support, rather than competition. Human beings may die alone, but only in rare instances do they live alone.

3. Increasing centralization of political and economic activity tends to undercut the health of smaller communities and the experience of social obligation and accountability that arise when people feel commitment to specific others. Decentralizing political and economic institutions is essential to a restoration of smaller human associations.

4. We need to develop or reclaim meaning systems that direct our attention to who we are rather than what we have. Such meaning systems should be aimed at supporting the health of the communities in which we are embedded, as well as enabling us to accept our place within a universe in which change and death are inevitable.

Following the pattern of Chapter 2, I discuss these assumptions in more detail. In the next chapter I consider the educational implications of this worldview, some existing educational models or theories that may facilitate its dissemination, and the role educators might play in fostering the development of a culture predicated upon it.

Identification Rather Than Detached Objectivity

One of the most fundamental aspects of the emerging world-view is its rejection of the Cartesian dualism between mind and matter (Capra, 1983; Coates, 1981; Devall, 1980; D'Souza, 1989; King, 1989; Oliver and Gershman, 1989; Smith, 1982). As will be recalled, this division has permitted those who have accepted the modern/industrial worldview to perceive the natural world as a collection of discrete and unrelated objects, or as Martin Buber (1958) would have said, a collection of *Its* with which we have no personal relationship. From this perspective, the universe has no more meaning or life than a machine. Meaning is found only in that which can reflect upon physical reality. Such reflection can be enhanced by looking not at wholes but at the component parts of the world around us. Through the investigation of those parts we can acquire knowledge of natural laws that will lead to mastery of the external environment.

In contrast to this orientation to the natural world and our knowledge of it is an orientation that emphasizes identification rather than detached observation, or to use Buber's terminology again, the establishment of an *I-Thou* relationship rather than an *I-It* relationship (cited in Coates, 1981, 25; Devall, 1980, 309). Such a perspective does not require the elimination of the forms of knowledge generated by contemporary science, but rather the integration of this knowledge into a more comprehensive vision of components embedded within wholes. In the following passage, quoted at length because of its description of the nature of relations grounded in an experience of interdependence rather than detachment, Buber contrasts these alternative approaches to the world:

I CONSIDER A TREE.

I can look on it as a picture: stiff column in a shock of light, or splash of green shot with the delicate blue and silver of the background.

I can perceive it as movement: flowing veins on clinging, pressing pith, suck of the roots, breathing of the leaves, ceaseless commerce with earth and air—and the obscure growth itself.

I can classify it in a species and study it as a type in its structure and mode of life.

I can subdue its actual presence and form so sternly that I recognise it only as an expression of law—of the laws in accordance with which a constant opposition of forces is continually adjusted, or of those in accordance with which the component substances mingle and separate.

I can dissipate it and perpetuate it in number, in pure numerical relation.

In all this the tree remains my object, occupies space and time, and has its nature and constitution.

It can, however, also come about, if I have both will and grace, that in considering the tree I become bound up in relation to it. The tree is now no longer *It*. I have been seized by the power of exclusiveness.

To effect this it is not necessary for me to give up any of the ways in which I consider the tree. There is nothing from which I would have to turn my eyes away in order to see, and no knowledge that I would have to forget. Rather is everything, picture and movement, species and type, law and number, indivisibly united in this event.

Everything belonging to the tree is in this: its form and structure, its colours and chemical composition, its intercourse with the elements and with the stars, are all present in a single whole.

The tree is no impression, no play of my imagination, no value depending on my mood; but it is bodied over against me and has to do with me, as I with it—only in a different way. (1958, 7–8)

Though some may object that such an approach to an experience of the world is essentially "mystical" rather than practical, the mystical elements of this approach may be nothing more than an expansion of scientific inquiry to include all aspects of the tree and its situation, including the observer. Buber's emphasis on the nature of the relationship between observer and observed and the development of a more holistic rather than partial perspective can in fact be encountered in the work of some scientific investigators.

Geneticist Barbara McClintock, a Nobel prizewinner, is one of these. McClintock does not reject elements of the research methodology encountered in modern science. She does, however, integrate it into her own intuited experience of more comprehensive wholes. For McClintock, her investigation of chromosomal patterns has not been aimed at the discovery of atomistic mechanical components, as was the case with the discoverers of DNA and RNA.[1] She has instead been concerned about understanding the way in which organisms interact as members of larger environmental contexts. The process by which she has uncovered the nature of this interrelationship has often been highly subjective and mysterious, rather than objective and rational. She describes her discovery of the cytology of the fungus neurospora in the following way:

> I found that the more I worked with them the bigger and bigger [they] got, and when I was really working with them I wasn't outside, I was down there. I was part of the system. I was right down there with them, and everything got big. I even was able to see the internal parts of the chromosomes—actually everything was there. It surprised me because I actually felt as if I were right down there and these were my friends. (in Keller, 1983, 117)

McClintock's most important work has involved the study of genetic patterns in corn. In this research as well, she emphasizes the importance of becoming intimate with rather than detached from the object of her study.

> I start with the seedling, and I don't want to leave it. I don't feel I really know the story if I don't watch the plant all the way along. So I know every plant in the field. I know them intimately, and I find it a great pleasure to know them. (in Keller, 1983, 198)

It is the possibility of such intimacy and identification that underlies the "deep" ecological thinking of Norwegian philosopher, Arne Naess (1985). Naess, as well as others associated with the deep ecology movement (Devall, 1980; Devall and Sessions, 1985), argues that the environmental crisis has been predicated at least in part on a failure of contemporary humans to identify with the world around them. Instead, many have become preoccupied with a narrow concept of self-realization, a process that often neglects a recognition of the broader *gestalts* within which the individual self is located. Naess suggests that this preoccupation has contributed to our alienation from one another and the natural world. By broadening our definition of the self to include more of that *gestalt*, however, he believes we will become more sensitive to the systemic consequences of our actions.

Feminists involved with the environmental movement have suggested that more than a narrow conception of self-realization has contributed to our detachment from the natural world. They point out that the patriarchal forms of domination that characterize the relations between men and women are replicated in the relationship between men and the environment. What needs to be challenged is this proclivity for domination. As Ynestra King writes,

> The ecology movement, in theory and practice, attempts to speak for nature—the "other" that has no voice and is not conceived of subjectively in our civilization. Feminism represents the refusal of the original "other" in patriarchal human society to remain silent or to be the "other" any longer. Its challenge of social domination extends beyond sex to social domination of all kinds, because the domination of sex, race, and class and the domination of nature are mutually reinforcing. (1989, 20)

A recognition of our identification with rather than detachment from the environment that surrounds us must thus call into question the modern/industrial attempt to "master" nature for human ends, particularly when that mastery is projected to lead to the death of a million species by the year 2000 (Naess, 1985, 269). As we are learning now, the destruction that has accompanied such mastery has a way of returning to our own homes and bodies. Rather than continuing to act as heedless developers, we may need to begin acting as prudent stewards, considering not only current human needs but the health of the biosphere over generations.

It is important to note, however, that an acceptance of this perspective on the nature of economic activity and development does not require the abandonment of technology (Coates, 1981, 24). Technology, rather, could serve as an important vehicle for the creation of more environmentally sound strategies for the meeting of fundamental human needs. Technology could conceivably support rather than work against the broader systemic processes in which human beings are embedded (Devall, 1980, 311, 313; King, 1983, 125; Schumacher, 1973). These technologies would ideally be small-scale and accessible to decentralized local communities generally more able than distant bureaucrats to weigh the impact of their economic activities upon the surrounding environment (Mewes, 1985, 17).

At the core of a recognition of our relationship to the natural world, however, must be more than a concern about the development of less exploitive technologies. We must also recognize that limited resources necessarily demand limited consumption (Bahro, 1986; Durning, 1991; Heilbroner, 1980). Only by accepting such limits will we be able to guard the well-being of future generations. Such an acceptance must result in altered expectations about standards of living and material comfort. This does not mean that we must accept the forms of deprivation encountered among economically disadvantaged populations today. If we husband rather than waste resources, we may well have the technological means to provide adequately for the basic needs of all people (Lappe and Collins, 1977). Doing so, however, will require that those who have much govern and redirect their desires so that those who have little will be able to live. Since from a relative standpoint, those with much now include a majority of residents of the developed nations, the difficulty of effecting this cultural transformation should not be underestimated. Some of the social dynamics that may contribute to the accomplishment of this end are discussed in the following section.

In summary, the adoption of an epistemological stance of "identification with" rather than "detachment from" may be a critical component of our transition to a culture able to recognize and accept limitations imposed upon human activities by the natural world. Such a stance does not require the rejection of the techniques and perspectives of modern science, although it will require us to recognize the limitations of detached objectivity and traditional research methods. Findings derived from an investigation of component parts must be seen as no more than one factor in an understanding of systemic wholes. Furthermore, our recognition of our own relationship to broader systems should enable us to grasp the importance of regulating our activities in ways that sustain rather than disrupt the health of those systems.

Cooperation Rather Than Possessive Individualism

The assumption that humanity stands in an interdependent rather than detached relationship with the physical universe parallels another fundamental assumption encountered in the alternative worldview under discussion here. This is that individual security and health are best served when people acknowledge and act upon their fundamental interdependence with one another. Such a perspective is significantly different from that shared by those who espouse the modern/industrial worldview. As noted in Chapter 2, during our own era individuals have been seen as isolated social atoms in competition with one another for the basic requirements of their own survival. The social networks into which they are born or choose to live have been generally viewed as secondary or even as impediments to the realization of this end. In contrast to this position, representatives of the new worldview see cooperation rather than competition as an essential component of the society that must replace our own if we are to adapt successfully to changed material conditions (Bahro, 1986; Boggs, 1986; Capra, 1983; Green Party of Federal Republic of Germany, 1985; Ophuls, 1977; Sale, 1985).

This element of the alternative worldview has been poorly theorized and is often based upon wishful thinking about the restoration of premodern societies (e.g., see Bahro's (1986) call for a return to self-sufficient quasi-monastic communities of approximately 2000 residents). Modern preoccupations shared by both the right and left about the pursuit of self-interest and/or self-development, however, provide a weak conceptual basis for the establishment of a way of life that directs peoples' attention to the needs of the collective. If occupational opportunities in developed nations become narrowed as a result of declines in productivity, competition for the increasingly elusive benefits of industrial society are likely to intensify. It seems probable that a market society will remain functional only as long as a majority of people are able to provide for themselves by participating in it. If they are not able to do so, they may turn to forms of support antithetical to the maintenance of social order and the rules of the market, itself.

Such a situation is now evident in the increasingly violent drug trade that has become a dominant feature of American inner cities. A market response to this situation would be for the state to assume an increasingly active role in suppressing activities that threaten public order. If illegal economic behaviors become more widespread, a likely possibility as the forces of production are reduced, there will come a point at which the maintenance of order will require increasingly extreme measures (e.g., the declaration of martial law) that could well threaten other social values.

An alternative response, one ignored by Hobbes and most contemporary political leaders, would be to recognize that for millenia human communities have developed indigenous patterns of cooperation that allowed them to establish social order and maintain a degree of economic stability without the intervention of an external institution like the modern state.[2] If during the next decades a reduction in the forces of production limits the ability of citizens to provide for themselves, it may be prudent to consider the utility of cooperative rather than competitive forms of economic support. In this way we might be able to diminish or avoid the social chaos or governmental repression that is likely to accompany the development of a bipolar class system that will almost certainly arise as restricted economic opportunity erodes the size of the middle class.

Outside the context of nuclear families, however, such forms of cooperative support are becoming increasingly rare in the United States. Martin Deutsch (1962), a social psychologist whose theoretical work on the nature of cooperative and competitive behavior forms the basis of Johnson and Johnson's (1974) cooperative learning strategies, would describe the interaction of individuals in a market society as being *contriently interdependent*. In such situations, the success of one person contributes to the failure of another (276). Although this portrayal of the market more accurately describes social relations encountered during the phase of entrepreneurial rather than corporate capitalism, the competitive ethic and the ideology of possessive individualism encountered during that earlier era remain profoundly influential in American life (Bellah et al., 1985).

In contrast to the contrient interdependence encountered within the market, efforts to establish forms of security that arise from collective rather than individual activity must be constructed upon what Deutsch has called *promotive interdependence*. Promotive interdependence specifies "a condition in which individuals are so linked together that there is a positive correlation between their goal attainment" (1962, 176). Promotive interdependence is often a feature of life in premodern societies and communities that continue to exist on the margins of our own civilization where individual welfare is dependent upon cooperative activities.[3] In these settings, nonmarket exchanges in the form of gift giving and shared labor establish patterns of obligation and support that function as an important social insurance against economic hardship. One thinks, for example, of the collective support found in Amish communities, where residents contribute their labor and resources to one another in ways that guarantee the well-being of all residents of the community. The Amish have gone so far as to reject both modern agricultural equipment and Social Security payments on the premise that a reliance upon such inventions could diminish their own sense of responsibility to one another (Hostetler, 1963).

Even in nonreligious communities, such cooperation is often evident. In his study of communal support in a series of West Virginia mining towns, Erikson (1976) notes the degree to which neighboring families of Appalachians had developed patterns of mutual aid that contributed to their experience of security in a difficult physical and economic environment. Such aid took the form of generous donations of money and food, as well as time, whenever neighbors encountered events that threatened their well-being, such as illness, unemployment, or deaths in the family.[4]

Similar forms of support are encountered among numerous populations around the globe where the survival of individuals has been dependent upon the existence of social patterns of obligation and mutual aid. After a thorough review of literature on social and economic relations in a number of premodern societies, Radin (1953), for example, has argued that

> irrespective of whether society is socially stratified or unstratified, democratic or monarchical, or whether the food-economy is that of the food-gatherer, the hunter-fisher, the agriculturalist or the pastoral-nomad, all aboriginal peoples accept the theory that every human being has the inalienable right to an irreducible minimum, consisting of adequate food, shelter, and clothing. (106)

Membership within the group was the only requirement for physical support. Gans (1962), Stack (1975), Johnson (1973), and Steinetz and Solomon (1986) have described the persistence of such patterns even in contemporary urban environments among ethnic minorities who have yet to set aside the social patterns they have inherited from what are, in effect, premodern villages.

For many Americans, however, traditional patterns of cooperative behavior and mutual aid have become vestigial. Increased personal wealth has diminished the necessity to turn to others for economic support. Since the personal costs of that support often included the obligation of reciprocity and the requirement to abide by group-determined standards of behavior, when individuals have been given the opportunity not to cooperate, they have chosen to create their own security rather than rely upon others (Erikson, 1976; Gans, 1962, 1988; Stack, 1975; Weis, 1985). The opportunity to make this choice, however, has depended upon the economic expansion that has occurred over the previous four centuries. There is a great danger that if and when economic conditions worsen, our minimal experience with cooperative behaviors will make it difficult for us to reinstitute patterns of support that may be essential for our well-being. With resources that may well be inadequate to provide for basic human support, our society could degenerate into the forms of predation and survivalism observed by Banfield (1958) and Turnbull (1972) in seriously impoverished communities. Avoiding this situation could require us to direct our attention once more to the needs of the community, rather than the pursuit of our own self-interest.

Decentralization as a Key to the Restoration of Cooperation

In his study of the nature of cooperation, Deutsch has argued that individuals will enter into cooperative forms of interaction in certain social circumstances rather than others. Such interaction is more likely to occur when individuals know one another, see themselves as an entity with common interests, and view cooperation as the most effective and attractive of available alternative forms of action (1962, 291). What is striking about these descriptors is the degree to which they are atypical of many social settings in industrial societies. Transcending our proclivity to act as possessive individuals will require doing more than developing alternatives to the market relations that have come to dominate our own society. We must as well address social and institutional patterns that inhibit the experience of promotive interdependence.

In the United States, for example, the neighborhoods and communities in which people once were able to develop a sense of social bondedness have become increasingly rare. Bedroom communities, shopping centers, mobility, the automobile, and private forms of entertainment have accentuated the anomie and isolation linked by Durkheim to modernization nearly a century ago. Although some churches, synagogues, schools, workgroups, and neighborhoods may provide an experience of group identity, most of us spend our lives associating with strangers or acquaintances with whom we feel little, if any, connection. What has been neglected in the process of creating ever-larger institutions in modern societies is the difficulty people have in experiencing a sense of identification with or responsibility toward others with whom they possess little personal knowledge or relationship.

Even if the opportunities to become known to one another were made available to us, however, the transference of economic and political authority away from peripheral villages and towns to urban centers has reduced the reason for even entering into cooperative relations. As Vidich and Bensman (1968) noted over 20 years ago in their study of a small town in central New York State, local citizens now have virtually no control over the decisions that bear most directly upon their lives. Economically and politically, those decisions are made in statehouses, Washington, D.C., or in the offices of distant corporate executives. In such a situation, cooperative activities can have little effect on personal security. Yet it is just this effect that appears essential if people are to become willing to enter into activities that will contribute to collective rather than individual welfare.

In recognition of these dynamics, writers now attempting to articulate the emerging worldview considered here point to the importance of creating smaller human settlements within which residents are given major control over their own political and economic lives (Bookchin, 1980; Capra and Spretnak, 1984; Devall, 1980; Green Party of Federal Republic of Germany, 1985; King, 1983; Mewes, 1985; Porritt, 1984; Sale, 1985; Salleh, 1984; Satin, 1987). A decentralization of economic and political authority away from urban and industrial centers could begin to help restore cooperative relations within smaller human associations and contribute to the belief that local activities can enhance individual and collective security. In regard to these issues, Sale (1985) has written:

> The only way people will apply "right behavior" and behave in a responsible way is if they have been persuaded to see problems concretely and to understand their own connections to them directly—and this can be done only at a limited scale. It can be done where the forces of government and society are still recognizable and comprehensible, where relations with other people are still intimate, and where the effects of individual actions are visible; where abstractions and intangibles give way to the here and now, the seen and felt, the real and known. (53)

For Sale, as well as many spokespeople for the emerging worldview, such decentralization takes the form of what is called bioregionalism. This political and economic vision attempts to spell out the implications of a devolution of power back to loosely federated local communities, which, like communities before the advent of modern transportation systems, would assume major responsibility for governing and providing for themselves. Although on one level such a vision seems impractical and unrealizable, if we remember that within 50 to 100 years the exhaustion of petroleum reserves could make most current forms of transportation obsolete, then bioregionalism seems more like an inevitability than a romantic dream. Furthermore, a serious economic downturn is likely to inhibit the ability of large nation-states and multinational corporations to continue to finance their own operations. If this perspective is accepted, then our task is to attempt to minimize the trauma that may accompany a transition to what may be unavoidable.

A current example of bioregionalism in action can be found in the Basque region of Spain. There, the Mondragon cooperatives demonstrate the potential creativity, intelligence, and energy that can be tapped through the development of structures that further grass-roots democracy and worker control of economic production. It may be through the cultivation of this kind of collective strength that we will be able to adjust to the new material realities that appear to await us. A brief description of the Mondragon organization follows:

> Mondragon is an association of nearly 200 enterprises (mostly industrial factories which manufacture durable goods, intermediate goods, and capital equipment, as well as producing electronic and high technology products), schools, and farms owned and managed by over 20,000 owners, who are also the only workers. They have guaranteed jobs for life, fully adequate take-home incomes, nearly equal participation in their firms' profits and losses, equal shares in the democratic control of their enterprises, broad health insurance plans for their families, a private unemployment program which pays 80% of take-home pay if they are ever laid off, and a pension program which pays 60% of their salary from the last day of work until death. (Mollner, 1988, 58)

Mondragon now includes Spain's top manufacturers of domestic appliances, machine tools, and industrial machinery. Its 100 commercial enterprises sold nearly $1 billion worth of goods and services in 1986 (Mollner, 1988, 58).

What seems significant about the Mondragon organization is its commitment to the development of an economic process whose aim is the creation of more owner-worker jobs. It accomplishes this end not through the development of competitive relations but through mutual investment on the part of its members in the economic efforts of others. This development is encouraged through the establishment of Mondragon banks, an entrepreneurial organization, a long-range research institute, a health and social security system, and a democratically controlled educational system. In this social and economic experiment, the effort of owner-workers is linked to the activities of a broad-based organization that turns cooperation into clearly realizable benefits for its members. Individuals are not left alone as they attempt to compete in the market but instead pool their resources in ways that contribute to the success of others.

This cooperative venture exemplifies the problem-solving potential that inheres in groups of people who now are often denied access to conventional channels of economic and political power. Though the health of the cooperative enterprises that compose Mondragon could well be jeopardized by a reduction in the forces of production, the lessons learned by its members about shared governance and collective support could put them in a good position to adjust to whatever the requirements posed by altered material conditions may be. For example, during the European business recession in the late 1970s and early 1980s, other firms fired 20 percent of their employees. Mondragon companies increased their employment by 36 percent (Mollner, 1988, 58).

I do not mean to imply by this description of the Mondragon cooperatives that a process of decentralization will make an adjustment to the end of the previous era of economic expansion easy. That adjustment will almost without question be difficult and dangerous. What Mondragon demonstrates, however, is that when provided with appropriate governance structures and the ability to realize jointly determined goals, groups of people on a local level are capable of governing their own lives with skill and responsibility. It is this collective entrepreneurialism that could be nurtured by decentralizing the authority of political and economic institutions currently aimed at furthering and controlling the interests and activities of possessive individuals.

In summary, the transformation in material conditions that may be precipitated by the environmental crisis and resource depletion is likely to make obsolete possessive individualism and the political and economic centralization that now characterize modern/industrial societies. To replace the forms of competition and impersonal governance now encountered in most modern nations, we will need to consider the adoption of an alternative outlook on the relationship between the individual and community, one that furthers cooperation and local control. By acting collectively rather than individually, it may be possible to achieve an acceptable level of physical security for the majority, rather than for what may become an increasingly small minority. Accomplishing this end will not be easy, for those who now have much will be unlikely to relinquish their own comfort and privilege without resistance. By failing to effectuate such a transition, however, we may run the risk of becoming a nation in which a small class maintains its own well-being by deceiving and/or repressing the majority.

The Development of New Meaning Systems: Choosing Community over Accumulation

In Chapter 2, I noted that one of the central assumptions of the modern/industrial worldview is that humanity lives in the context of a linear time frame within which we expect to enjoy increasing levels of material progress as we advance into the future. This belief in a forward-moving rather than cyclical temporal process is not unique to modernization—it is also a central component of the Messianic traditions in both Judaism and Christianty. Since the sixteenth century, however, the forward movement of time has been the object of a material rather than spiritual interpretation. Perhaps one of the most profound challenges presented by a reduction in the forces of production to those who subscribe to the modern/industrial worldview is the possibility that the ideology of progress, itself, is an illusion (Lasch, 1989). Although some intellectuals have consistently questioned the merits of modernization throughout the twentieth century, their voices have generally been lost in the rush to technological innovation and increased affluence. Their warnings certainly have not been heeded by most citizens of the industrialized world nor their governors.

If the environmental crisis proves to be as serious as it now appears, however, more people may come to believe that the modern faith in the possibility of secular salvation—via either capitalism or socialism—has been misplaced. As this happens, it may become imperative to provide an alternative system of meaning to which they can attach their lives, a system of meaning that acknowledges the unavoidable limitations imposed by the planet upon the expression of human ideas and creativity. Like the preceding assumptions about personalized rather than detached forms of knowledge, cooperation rather than possessive and competitive individualism, and decentralization, a concern about the nature of a meaning system that could replace the ideology of progress is encountered in the writings of a number of people who are attempting to articulate the dimensions of the emerging worldview.

In *Beyond the Post-Modern Mind* (1982), for example, Huston Smith suggests that the modern compulsion to control the external world as a means for achieving material progress has directed our attention away from what may be more fundamental human concerns about personal change, maturity, and mortality. He contrasts our desire for control with the desire for participation encountered in earlier societies. This participation, linked to an epistemology that valued intuitive discernment and a worldview that saw life in transcendent rather than purely natural terms contributed to the experience of fulfillment (143–44). It is exactly this fulfillment that is often absent in our quest for increasing material comfort and security, since in the end neither wealth nor comfort can protect us from our own deaths.

Coates (1981) argues that in contrast to the focus on improving the material conditions of life, those who subscribe to what he calls the "metaindustrial paradigm" believe that "the goal of human existence is self-transformation" and that the achievement of this goal is furthered by keeping material goods to a minimum. Instead of gaining meaning through the possession of objects, that meaning is gained through our transcendence of "small and limited egos" (p 26). As indicated earlier, Naess (1985) similarly points to a vision of maturity that involves not accumulation but a deepening identification with other beings. Through that identification, people will come to act with a greater degree of responsibility and accountability toward the well-being of others.

It is this opportunity for relatedness and mutuality that psychologist Paul Wachtel (1988) in his book, *The Poverty of Affluence*, holds up as an alternative to material accumulation. He argues that the modern/industrial worldview has denied what appears to be a deep human desire to be "part of something." If we can once again be given the chance to experience a sense of identification and participation with others, the pleasure and security we receive as a result of more fulfilling relationships may be enough to encourage us to set aside our expectations for ever-increasing abundance and comfort. We may become more willing to live simply, with less, if doing so is linked to living in community with others in ways that answer more completely our need for security and belonging. By appealing to this deeper need, a need unanswered by the scientific and social architects of modernity, it may be possible to encourage residents of the industrialized West to turn away from their allegiance to a worldview that has become dysfunctional and adopt another more likely to support, rather than destroy, life on this planet.

Achieving this end, however, will require overcoming traditional social patterns of rising expectations that could well be irresistible. Yet it is these expectations that will need to be replaced if we are to establish a culture that sustains rather than erodes the environment upon which we depend for our existence. I have no illusions about the difficulty inherent in disseminating and then cultivating an alternative meaning system that focuses on the importance of personal maturation and transformation rather than the acquistion of wealth and the achievement of physical comfort. As human communities are faced with increasingly difficult economic challenges, however, individuals may have no choice but to locate their sense of meaning in a vision of progress that has little to do with material accumulation and more to do with the quality of their relations with other people and the broader environment.

Conclusion

Before moving on to a consideration of the role that educators might play in fostering a worldview that emphasizes sustainability, it may be useful to conclude this section with a brief illustration of what a society founded upon the preceding principles might look like. First, it would be a society in which natural limits are respected and human beings seek to live their lives in ways that nurture, rather than jeopardize, the ecological systems that support them. Respect for these limits would be encouraged by helping children and adults to acknowledge their membership in surrounding nonhuman communities and to recognize that their own interests lie in the preservation rather than exploitation of the natural environment. Both old and new technologies within this society would be carefully evaluated on the basis of their potential impact on the environment, with environmental concerns being given precedence over economic possibilities. The primary aim of the economy, itself, would be the fulfillment of basic human needs for shelter, nourishment, and health care, rather than the multiplication of creature comforts.

Second, relations in a society based upon the alternative worldview would foster cooperation and diminish the opportunities for economic competition among its members. Physical well-being would not depend upon performance in a marketplace in which individual support was solely predicated upon the possession of desirable attributes and talents. This does not mean that either talent or achievement would be discouraged, however. They would instead be cultivated within the context of face-to-face groups whose security would depend upon the efforts and commitment of their members. These groups could be constructed around a variety of principles. Kin, locale, occupation, religious inclination—all might be used as the basis for establishing these smaller associations. What is most important is that individuals would no longer believe that their security and support depended solely upon their own performance in an impersonal economic environment. As in the Mondragon cooperatives, membership and responsible participation would guarantee support.

Because the success and longevity of such cooperative associations would almost certainly depend upon their ability to contribute to the security of their members, economic and political power within a society based upon the emerging worldview would be decentralized into smaller governmental units that would strive toward the goal of economic self-reliance. Such units could be based upon bioregional characteristics. These units, like the communities and smaller human associations found within them, would be set within larger federations of bioregions whose aim would be the coordination of activities and resolution of conflict between smaller units. Although the specifics of this form of economic and political decentralization have yet to be spelled out with clarity, what is perhaps most important about whatever model is developed is the provision of broadly based citizen participation in policymaking that impinges upon communal security.

Finally, within the context of these ecologically responsible, cooperative, and decentralized communities, people would seek their sense of meaning and identity through the maintenance of mutually supportive relations with one another, as well as through explorations of their place within an interdependent and interactive universe. Buddhist philosophers have suggested that the cosmos is like a net in which each being is a jewel which reflects all other beings. This vision is not dissimilar from the vision of interdependence presented by the science of ecology. Predicated upon a recognition of such interdependence or interbeing, the cultural ideal of such a society would not be the attainment of wealth, but the living of a life that sustains rather than sunders relationships.

At first reading, such a vision may appear unrealistic and utopian. It is important to remember, however, that with the exception of a handful of imperial civilizations prior to the modern era, human beings have lived for millenia in settings that to one extent or another resembled the social order described here more than that encountered in our own society. It has been within the context of such communities that our species has been able to persist. Furthermore, I have not suggested that this social vision would be free of conflict or suffering. Struggles between and within these smaller social units could well be inevitable. In addition, it seems likely that the forms of greed, aggression, and elitism that underlie the development of class societies will continue to lead to discrimination and domination. Despite these problems, however, a society based upon a recognition of natural limits, cooperation, interpersonal commitments, and a sense of mutual identification seems less dangerous to the welfare of our species than does our own top-heavy, alienating, and environmentally destructive civilization. Our best hope may lie in acknowledging the fact that the assumptions that underlie the modern/industrial worldview have brought us to our current impasse and that those assumptions need to be replaced by others that more accurately reflect the nature of current material conditions. Any alternative vision is likely to possess serious flaws, but these flaws may be less damaging than those that are now contributing to the erosion of the natural and social systems upon which our lives depend. At issue now is how such a vision might be brought from the margins of our society into the center. And it is here that educators may have some role to play.

Five

❂

Shaping Schools for a
Sustainable Society

An educational model capable of transmitting and confirming the worldview discussed in the previous chapter would draw children into the lived experience of interrelatedness and away from the detached independence currently cultivated in contemporary classrooms. As the pursuit of self-interest is impeded by the limits of the planet, we will have to regenerate patterns of mutual support encountered in premodern societies and affirm ways of knowing that acknowledge our membership in the broad natural and social ecological systems of which we are a part. The cultivation of such support and the acknowledgment of this membership will require the creation of educational practices and structures that impart a new hidden curriculum, one that nurtures interdependence, achievement for the well-being of the group, affective and particularistic ties, and a deep sense of moral responsibility to the natural environment and to one another. Such an education would acknowledge the importance of ties to primary groups, build upon ways of knowing that balance interaction and identification with detached objectivity, encourage cooperation and collective responsibility, and foster forms of decision making and governance that support the welfare of the entire community, rather than its privileged sectors.

If it is agreed that the regular structures, instructional practices, and content of most classrooms and schools synergistically act as powerful socializing agents that induct children into the modern/industrial worldview, then the development of schools capable of inducting children into a sustainable worldview will require modifying those regularities. The first section of this chapter discusses the nature of those modifications. It is important to note that many of the practices discussed can in fact be encountered in existing educational programs. They are not widespread, but most are also not untried. The chapter notes direct interested readers to more extensive descriptions of schools using these practices. The second section briefly reviews the work of selected educational theoreticians who have also called for the creation of an educational process capable of reversing some of the socially disintegrative aspects of modern society. This discussion is not meant to be comprehensive, but rather suggestive. Although none of these writers has dealt with all the factors I raise here, each has touched on different elements of the educational model that arise from my analysis. Although their suggestions have found little favor in the United States, insights drawn from their work could help us to reshape schools in ways more appropriate for the conditions we are likely to encounter during the coming decades.

Schooling for Interdependence

Creating schools that affirm students' attachment to others and the natural environment and which teach them to act collectively will require the systematic disassembling and reformulation of elements of the hidden curriculum described in Chapter 3. Although accomplishing this task will be a critical first step in the development of schools capable of at least partially socializing children in the direction I have laid out here, it should not be assumed that altering the hidden curriculum will alone be enough to ground them in a new worldview. Elements of the explicit curriculum will also need to be changed. Courses in conflict resolution, ecological principles, peace studies, group dynamics, systems theory, global environmental trends, and multicultural studies, for example, could also contribute to this end. It goes without saying that other elements in the broader social environment, such as child-rearing practices and mass communication, will also need to be altered to ensure such a transformation. For our present purposes, however, I will continue to focus primarily on structural and pedagogical considerations because I believe it is in regard to these elements, rather than intellectual course work, that educators can play their most important role in shaping children's worldview and social habits.

Restoring the Experience of Interdependence

Enabling children to grasp and live out their interdependence with others and the natural world will require us to develop educational forms that are set as much as possible within the communities from which students come. Instead of physically separating children from those communities, as is generally the case now, educators must strive to create learning experiences that break beyond the boundaries of the classroom and root themselves in the broader environment. One consequence of such efforts is that the line between school, home, workplace, and the natural world would become less defined. This could be accomplished through a variety of means.

A significant share of students' learning activities, for example, could take place beyond the school building within their own neighborhoods and local parks and wild areas. Children could be encouraged to bring their findings and observations back to their fellow-learners and to become the creators of knowledge rather than its consumers or passive observers. In this process, they could learn how to evaluate the quality and veracity of one another's work, as well as how to respect the efforts of others by knowing the costs and demands of such effort themselves. Local history and social studies projects, environmental studies, occupational internships, involvement in political action groups, community service, regular camping trips, and the maintenance of school gardens all could provide opportunities for students to experience learning in sites beyond the classroom.[1]

Bringing nonschool volunteers into the classroom is another means for diminishing the boundary between school and its broader context. Parents and grandparents, neighbors, local craftspeople and artists, bus drivers, policemen and policewomen, government officials, business people, and political activists, for example, could help children begin to interpret the world from their perspective as well as that of teachers and principals. They, too, could do much to overcome the isolation of schools from the broader environment in which they are set.[2]

Not only could schools be more closely set within the social and natural worlds of their students, they could also attempt to honor rather than supplant students' cultural traditions. This would mean that instead of utilizing the generic textbooks that now dominate most American classrooms, educators would strive to develop materials that more accurately represent the cultural backgrounds of their own students. Local as well as ethnic art, music, dance, literature, and food could be given a primary place in learning activities. This would not necessarily entail neglecting works associated with what has been viewed as the dominant Anglo-American culture; rather, these as well as works from other nonlocal traditions would be studied as representative of the cultural riches found in other particular places.

Although efforts should be made to avoid parochialism and narrow-
mindedness, grounding children within the culture of their own families and neighborhoods would be seen as a fundamental responsibility of educators. From that groundedness, children could then explore
the cultures of other groups.[3]

It must be acknowledged that for many American children,
especially those from middle-class suburban homes, significant family or local traditions have been all but erased by geographic mobility,
schooling, and the mass media. In this situation, educators may need
to take it upon themselves to reacquaint students with their own
roots, helping them to reconstruct their own stories by interviewing
parents and grandparents, reclaiming rituals and celebrations, and
learning again the folk tales and epics of the "tribes" from which they
originally came.

This is not to say that we should attempt to foster a balkaniza-
tion of American life; such a project would be counterproductive in a
world where intergroup strife is becoming increasingly dangerous if
not suicidal. The aim of helping children understand the historical
communities of which they are a part is to validate diversity and slow
if not reverse the dissemination of a modern monoculture that,
because of its ephemeral and nonlocal nature, has little power to win
the allegiance of people who consume it, and little power to create a
sense of collective identity or commitment (Eshete, 1982).

Although there is no way to return to the forms of cultural
diversity that continued to mark American life as late as World War
II, restoring a sense of place and people on a regional level could be
an important concomitant of the regeneration of communities capable
of collectively addressing the difficult economic and political changes
that lie ahead of us. When people share a commonly recognized history and at least some traditions and rituals, they are more likely to
experience the mutual identification that undergirds well-functioning
primary groups and small communities (Erikson, 1976).

It must be admitted that there are unavoidable risks in the reformulation of more clearly defined in-groups and out-groups—risks
that, in the forms of ethnic or religious conflict and racism, continue
to be problematic even in industrialized nations. This risk, however,
may be less dangerous than the social chaos or repression that could
arise in a society of isolated individuals competing for limited
resources. There are no easy answers to this dilemma, but that fact
should not deter us from attempting to grapple with this issue.

Beyond acquainting children with their own traditions and his-
tories, the development of instructional practices that demand

involvement and participation rather than detached withdrawal could also serve to induct students into the experience of interdependence. These practices would be based upon the premise that meaningful knowledge is personal and tied to experience. As indicated, extending the boundaries of the school would contribute to the implementation of this kind of experiential learning. Other alternative instructional practices that provide opportunities for student questions and inquiry, problem solving, decision making, and group projects would offer means for integrating this kind of involvement as well. By basing learning on students' own labor, thought, and sharing with peers, it would become part of their own life rather than the life of unknown others.[4]

Finally, in addition to providing a variety of settings in which students could master more instrumental forms of knowledge and skills, schools would affirm values related to the maintenance of the health of the communities in which they are embedded. Schooling would not be primarily directed toward individual benefit alone. It would also be aimed at developing a sense of social and environmental responsibility. Though not aligned with a particular creed, schools could unabashedly assert the values of tolerance, caring, land stewardship, honesty, commitment to meeting the needs of others, and nonviolence—values essential for the long-term well-being of any human community that intends to remain in the same place for more than a few generations.

While it is unrealistic to believe that all children exposed to such values would in fact incorporate them into their daily lives, it seems better for educators to try to achieve this end rather than give up the effort entirely. Children will acquire some values, even if they must create them on their own (Bernstein, 1975; Wax, Wax, and Dumont, 1964). If we want students to acquire those which appear to be critical to the maintenance of human communities, we may need actively to teach the values we see as desirable and create social settings in which they can be given expression.

Creating schools that connect students to their own communities and locale and which ground learning in personal rather than abstract knowledge may thus require introducing major changes in the ways educators conceive of the school and the very nature of instruction itself. Formal learning would ideally be seen as a process that could be located in multiple settings, both within the school and beyond it. Educators would seek to honor and cultivate the cultural traditions of their students in addition to acquainting them with the culture of other groups. They would utilize instructional practices that validate and extend, rather than replace, the forms of personal knowledge and experience children bring with them to school, and would strive to draw them into a set of values that contribute to the well-being of the varied communities in which they live. These strategies would be coupled to the creation of a school environment that furthers the development of supportive ties among adults and students within the school. It is to the nature of that environment that I turn next.

Developing Social Habits of Cooperation and Collective Responsibility

As the competitive activities of the market become less able to help individuals achieve a degree of personal security, the forms of social detachment associated with possessive individualism will become less useful or appropriate for a growing share of the population. The norms and social habits currently taught by the schools will then need to be replaced by others that enable children to learn the importance of linking their efforts to the efforts of others. Instead of independence, students will need to learn how to live interdependently, recognizing both the opportunities and limitations that arise from this altered perspective. Economically, such interdependence could be expressed through nonmarket forms of exchange such as barter, sharing, and gift-giving. Interdependence could also be expressed through the formation of cooperative rather than competitive occupational ventures.

Although educators will generally not be in a position to influence the economic behaviors students enter into outside the school, they could encourage the cultivation of social relations that foster collective well-being, rather than the detached and competitive relations generally encountered within most present schools. Accomplishing this end will undoubtedly require a variety of strategies, but one place to begin would be to alter some of the school's programmatic and behavioral regularities that inhibit such identification and interdependence.

As indicated in Chapter 3, students in school learn to interact with adults who behave in a distant and generally unsupportive manner. This situation is predicated in part on the fact that in most schools students outnumber adults by a significant margin. Although substantially reducing student/teacher ratios may not be within the realm of possibility, given budgetary restraints that will almost certainly accompany a reduction in the forces of production, steps could still be taken to ensure that children have more ongoing contact and support from adults within the school. The hiring of more paraprofessionals to work closely with teachers in classrooms is one strategy for accomplishing this end. The development of volunteer tutoring and mentoring programs is another way of increasing the amount of time students have to work with caring and interested adults. Involving all school staff in the supervision of advisory groups provides yet another means for linking children to adults in small enough groups to give students the assistance and support many of them need to feel connected to the school.[5]

More fundamental to the success of such programs, however, must be a deepening understanding that schools should not attempt to engender detached independence. This does not mean that teachers would leave children dependent on adult assistance to accomplish their own goals. They would instead strive to help students gain the competencies needed to contribute to their own social groups while providing a net of assistance and support. Such a net has not been a common feature in most classrooms where many of those who fail have not received the assistance and encouragement they require to become successful; too often, teacher support is shown to able students less in need of sustained assistance. The care and attention offered to the successful needs to be shared more universally.

One step toward achieving this end would be to lengthen the amount of time students remain with one teacher or group of teachers. Students, for example, might be assigned to the same adult(s) for a number of years, a practice encountered in a number of European countries, as well as Waldorf schools in the United States. This would give students and teachers the opportunity to form long-term relationships more like the relationships encountered within the home. One of the advantages of such a situation would be that both parties to this relationship would be more likely to develop commitments to one another that could diminish the need for the impersonal forms of social control often found in schools. Another advantage is that accountability for student learning would become clearly associated with one teacher or group of teachers. Student failure could not be blamed on a series of faceless and often forgotten individuals. Though this would not necessarily mean that all students would automatically become successful, just as children raised by concerned parents do not always develop in desired directions, it could lead to the more widespread provision of support and assistance.[6]

Finally, teachers could be encouraged to become more than instructors and to adopt a more personal and caring role with students. Accomplishing this end will involve at least two factors. First, time will need to be scheduled into the school day during which teachers would have the opportunity to counsel students and act more as concerned and helpful adults than as dispensers of information. Regular advisory periods such as those described earlier could provide such time. More important, however, moving beyond the narrowly limited role assumed by most educators, especially at the secondary level, will also require a willingness on the part of teachers to make themselves more available and vulnerable to their students. Teachers may need to become more attentive to the many factors that impinge upon the lives of children in their classrooms, and not simply those which relate to whether students are mastering the content presented in lectures and textbooks. Such a role contrasts in significant ways with the specific role most teachers have encountered or been taught as they have received their own education. Many social practices and habits will need to be unlearned, as well as learned. Again, however, if teachers keep in mind the necessity of forging relationships based upon the experience of interdependence, the process of making this shift may not be as difficult as it initially appears. Most of us have had the experience of being cared for and emotionally supported at one point or another in our lives; the task for teachers will be to apply what they encountered then to the patterns of interaction they establish with their own students.

Not only will students' relations with their teachers need to be altered; so, too, will their relations with one another. At the outset, it will be important for educators to acknowledge that students do form a community of interest that must be acknowledged and nurtured, rather than repressed or fragmented. Instead of attempting to resist this community in an effort to keep it at bay or under control, teachers will need to learn to work with their students collectively. This will necessitate giving students a broader role in shaping the conditions of their own classrooms and education. Participation in the process of creating and governing the learning environment could provide an important means for helping students acquire the social skills of cooperation, responsibility, and conflict resolution essential to the health of well-functioning communities.[7]

Such participation could also encourage a deeper sense of membership as students learn that involvement can result in changes they view as beneficial for both themselves and others. In social environments regulated primarily by others, individuals often emotionally withdraw when they realize that personal effort results in few changes in the nature of their situation. When involvement can lead to desirable ends, however, cooperation and interpersonal commitment become more likely (Deutsch, 1962).

This sense of membership and involvement is also more likely to arise when schools are small rather than large (Barker and Gump, 1964; Gregory and Smith, 1987). Either by creating smaller schools or by dividing large schools into schools-within-a-school, educators could overcome some of the anonymity and sense of interpersonal isolation that have come to characterize many contemporary educational institutions. These structural reforms could make it easier for students to experience a sense of social bonding with an identifiable group of peers with whom they share a variety of activities. Although smaller programs in themselves would not necessarily facilitate this outcome, the development of opportunities—both curricular and extracurricular—during which students could form interpersonal ties could lead to a stronger sense of affiliation and group membership among a larger proportion of the student body (Barker and Gump, 1964). The evolution of such affiliation and membership could be further facilitated by allowing students to remain not only with their teachers for a number of years, but with one another as well.[8]

Changes in the way children are scheduled within school could also contribute to their experience of interpersonal attachment. Rather than regarding students as social atoms to be assigned to classrooms simply on the basis of impersonal bureaucratic categories and convenience, school administrators could attempt to create "learning communities" composed of students who are already friends or who share common interests (Lipsitz, 1984). This could be especially important if larger schools are broken into schools-within-a-school. If close friends are separated, for example, this fact could impinge upon their own sense of relatedness to the school and their peers within the educational "clusters" to which they are assigned. Again, rather than disregarding interpersonal ties, as tends to be the case now, schools could honor those relationships and see them as the foundation upon which more extensive forms of student alliance could be built.

The formation of student ties could be further encouraged through the utilization of alternative instructional practices that require interaction rather than isolation. Instead of learning how to be alone within a crowd, students could be given ongoing opportunities to work with their peers on collective tasks. This would mean that the present emphasis on lectures, recitation, and individual seatwork would become secondary to pedagogical strategies that focus on cooperation and the completion of socially meaningful and valuable lessons. Learning in this situation would become essentially a social activity, in which students learn for one another rather than for themselves alone. Motivation would be based upon the sense of commitment and responsibility students feel toward their peers.[9] It must be acknowledged that cooperative learning has become a popular educational innovation in the late 1980s and early 1990s; such an approach, however, remains more the exception than the rule. Stigler and Stevenson's recent observations of more than 80 first- and fifth-grade classrooms in Minneapolis and Chicago revealed that children spent only 10 percent of their time working in small groups during the mathematics lessons that were the subject of their inquiry (1991, 17).

Encouraging cooperation, commitment, and responsibility could depend upon the development of alternative evaluation strategies based upon promotive rather than contrient forms of interdependence (Deutsch, 1962; Johnson and Johnson, 1974).[10] As long as many students believe that their own success depends upon doing better than their peers, they will be unlikely to offer one another the mutual support that often characterizes the relationships of people who share bonds of attachment. It must be admitted that such support, in the form of cheating, does occur in most schools. Cheating, however, is normally aimed at enhancing the welfare of small rather than larger student groups. By being surreptitious, the mutual support expressed in this way also fails to achieve legitimacy and is instead seen to be contrary to the norms valued by the larger society. If cooperation is to become legitimate, teachers will need to adopt evaluation strategies that reward contributions made to the group as well as individual achievement.

Changes in a number of behavioral and programmatic regularities within the school could thus lay the groundwork upon which more interdependent social relations could be constructed. Instead of the detached social relations encountered in most contemporary schools, educators would strive to create settings in which children can experience sustained and reliable adult support and join with their peers in working together toward the achievement of common goals. Altered patterns of school governance, scheduling policies, instructional practice, and evaluation procedures all could contribute to this end.

Before moving on to a consideration of strategies that might be adopted to bring about this transformation, it is important to recognize that many of the reforms suggested here have been part of the discourse regarding education throughout much of the twentieth century. Similar proposals have been presented by individuals primarily concerned about socially disintegrative aspects of the modern/industrial world. Although none of these people has considered the implications of the ideology of progress for the natural world in the way I have here, many have attempted to imagine an educational process capable of reversing some of the alienation, anomie, and lack of social integration that have accompanied modernization. In the final section of this chapter, I offer a brief overview of some of their ideas in an effort to place my own proposals within a broader historical and theoretical context.

Education for Social Interdependence: Other Models

Although there has been a general tendency to value the way public education has liberated children from "the constraints imposed by the accident of birth," as James Coleman and Thomas Hoffer (1987, xxvi) have observed, other voices have been raised over the past century about the dangers of attenuating fundamental social ties as children are prepared to take their place in a competitive market society. Educational models aimed at inducting children into the forms of social relation encountered in well-functioning primary groups have also been proposed and, on occasion, implemented. In the United States, however, few of these models have achieved much popularity or longevity.

The public's concern about individual achievement and adjustment to the requirements of life in a modern/industrial society have generally made such alternatives appear impractical or undesirable. Little has come of them. Whether more may come of them now seems likely to depend upon changes in our material conditions that could provide a more favorable environment for such experiments, an issue I deal with at greater length at the conclusion of this chapter. In what follows, I do not attempt to review all models of educational practice aimed at engendering a deeper sense of social membership and commitment; such a task would be worthy of a book in itself. I will, however, consider a set of proposals or experiments put forward by a number of educators who have specifically addressed the need to alter taken-for-granted elements of schools that have tended to diminish the strength of students' communal ties. These include John Dewey (1916/1966; 1927; 1929; 1959), Fred Newmann and Donald Oliver (1967), James Coleman and Thomas Hoffer (1987), Nel Noddings (1984), David and Roger Johnson (1974), Urie Bronfenbrenner (1970), Elizabeth Cagan (1978), and Mary Anne Raywid (1988).

Dewey was particularly sensitive to the erosion of small communities and the consequences of this process for the health of society as a whole. Much of his educational writing and his experiments at the University of Chicago's Lab School were directed toward finding ways by which children could be inducted into what he later came to call the Great Community (1927). He was afraid that the old individualism encountered in frontier America was being transmuted into a new individualism characterized by "pecuniary" preoccupations and limited social vision (1929). Dewey felt that unless children were helped to understand their place within the vast network of industrial occupations it would be difficult for them to become responsible and participating citizens in a modern democracy. It is for this reason that the curriculum at the Lab School focused as heavily as it did on a study of occupations (1959, 45–46). Dewey believed that by investigating and practicing skills related to cooking, textile manufacturing, carpentry, and agriculture children would come to understand the link between their own productive activities and the productive activities encountered in modern society. He felt that such an understanding was common in premodern communities but had been obscured as the home was replaced by the factory as the primary site of production. Furthermore, he argued that giving children an opportunity to direct their attention to the completion of common physical and social tasks would once more weld them into an embryonic community within which they would be able to see the social significance of their own actions (1959, 45). His hope was that after having encountered this form of communal membership within a controlled and supportive school environment, students would be able to transfer their understanding of interdependence to the broader society.

Although Dewey can be faulted for his failure to grapple with the difficulty of translating face-to-face relationships within a school to membership in a society that has become as abstract and impersonal as our own, his attempt to break down the division between the classroom and the broader community remains instructive. By following his lead, educators might begin to enable children to understand the nested social networks of which they are a part. Dewey's efforts to help children become responsible participants in school decision making also seem particularly important as a means for demonstrating interconnectedness and mutual responsibility (1916/1966).

In their attempt to narrow the gap between education and the communities in which it takes place, Newmann and Oliver (1967) have stressed that school should not be seen as the sole site of formal learning. Especially when students attempt to acquire the skills and knowledge associated with different occupations, crafts, or arts, a more appropriate learning context might be the laboratory, studio, or work environment. They have argued that it is in the company of nonprofessional teachers such as skilled workers, craftspeople, and artists that students should seek such learning. Newmann (1975) has further suggested that students will be more likely to learn the dispositions and skills required for responsible citizenship by becoming involved in decision making regarding specific issues encountered in their local community. Newmann's curriculum for citizenship competence directs students' attention to local issues they could potentially influence, such as the creation of bike trails or an increase in funding for women's athletics programs in their school. Ideally, students would work collectively to investigate dimensions of the policy issue they have chosen to study and become participants in the public debate regarding its implementation. This process includes a number of components: moral deliberation, social policy research, knowledge of the political-legal process, and the development of advocacy, group process, and organizational skills. Despite their different emphases regarding the location in which the development of a greater degree of communal membership might arise, Dewey as well as Oliver and Newmann offer clear suggestions about ways in which the forms of isolation, alienation, and meaninglessness that often typify conventional classrooms could be overcome. All have also stressed the value of student participation and involvement in the act of learning and of relating instructional activities to children's life experiences.

Coleman and Hoffer (1987) have more recently written of the interrelationship between students' academic success and the extent to which their schools are located in what they call functional communities. For Coleman and Hoffer, a functional community is composed of a number of families who share a similar set of values, generally live in proximity, and support one another in the rearing of their children. Within such communities, schools offer parents additional resources for educating the young that would be difficult to provide otherwise. In this situation, "The school is an institution of [the] community, the family is part of the community, and the child attends the school as a part of this functional community" (xxvi). They argue that the breakdown of such communities as a result of modernization is now inhibiting the effectiveness of conventional schools. In response, they suggest that efforts should be made to enhance the interrelationship between the school and the community through such measures as strengthening parent-teacher organizations, bringing adult volunteers into the schools through mentoring programs, actively sponsoring students who are experiencing academic failure, and placing schools within settings, such as the workplace, where teachers could establish closer relations with parents of children in the school. In this way, schools might be able to overcome some of the lack of social integration Coleman and Hoffer suggest lies behind the phenomena of educational failure and dropout.

Whereas the preceding authors have addressed their attention primarily to ways by which educators could diminish the boundary between school and community, the following have been more concerned about how the school itself might foster social relations based upon care, cooperation, and collective responsibility. Nel Noddings (1984), David and Roger Johnson (1974), Urie Bronfenbrenner (1970), and Elizabeth Cagan (1978) have all raised issues regarding the nature of the school's internal social environment and its impact on the sense of interrelatedness children experience toward one another.

Nel Noddings has addressed herself specifically to the way in which children's experience within schools can shape their ethical development. Of primary concern to Noddings is the cultivation of the ability to care and be cared for. From her viewpoint as a feminist, the maintenance of relationships resides at the core of ethical behavior. Perhaps more than any of the other authors cited here, Noddings has articulated what it means to ground our interaction with others and the world in a recognition of interdependence. For her, the primary aim of education must be to prepare children for "caring and being cared for in the human domain and full receptivity and engagement in the nonhuman world" (1984, 174).

To accomplish this end, she proposes a number of changes in the way we conceive of formal schooling and the relationship that exists between teachers and students. She insists, for example, that schools must be smaller if the experience of caring is to be cultivated in a sustained and conscientious manner. Furthermore, teachers and students must be given the opportunity to work with one another over extended periods of time in order to develop a sense of affiliation and attachment. From the perspective of ethical development, what is most important is "not the establishment of programs but the establishment and evaluation of chains and circles of caring" (180).

Within structures that support the experience of care, teachers must then strive to develop relations with their students that model what it means to be mutually supportive. She posits three ways to do this. First, teachers must invite students to participate in dialogues about critical issues in an effort to marry caring and thought. No subject should be excluded in the process because of its potential divisiveness. Instead, the school should be utilized as "a setting in which values, beliefs, and opinions can be examined both critically and appreciatively" (184). The aim of this process would be to enable students to "come into contact with ideas and to understand, to meet the other and to care" (186). In this way, sectarian divisions that might inhibit the evolution of caring communities could be overcome.

Second, students must be given the opportunity to demonstrate their care for others in concrete practice. Noddings suggests that schools be organized in ways that would allow students to participate with regularity in service activities. Whereas students would be expected to learn skills associated with work in agencies such as hospitals, nursing homes, or animal shelters, the primary purpose of these activities would be to cultivate their competence as people able to care for others. The development of these service experiences and internships would, furthermore, draw more adults into the educational act, demonstrating, as Noddings says, that "[E]ducation is an enterprise in which all of us should be engaged" (188). Students' experience of subject matter should also be personalized in a concrete and immediate manner, in an effort to help students encounter knowledge of the world in the way that Buber encountered the tree described earlier— "as that which will seize and delight them" (Noddings, 1985, 192). Relatedness and caring, rather than detachment, should thus infuse students' educational experiences within the school.

Finally, Noddings argues that teachers must not allow the evaluation strategies they adopt to measure learning to interfere with their primary obligation to students: the maintenance of a caring relationship. She suggests that at the heart of the intellectual experience of teaching and learning is the teacher's confirmation of the child's growing mastery and competence. This process must be informed by both high expectations and realism. One way to accomplish this end is to make evaluation a cooperative process in which the student is encouraged to demonstrate his or her own best effort. The student as well as the teacher then becomes a party to evaluation. Grading in such a situation is not something that is done to the student but with him or her. Evaluation, like dialogue and practice, can then serve to nurture in the student an ever-deepening recognition of relatedness and interdependence.

The use of cooperative learning strategies can also foster the experience of relatedness. David and Roger Johnson have been active and articulate proponents of cooperative education in the U.S. because of its beneficial effects on student achievement and its role as an antidote to stress. They argue, for example, that children learn more effectively when they are able to teach one another, something which is a common feature of cooperative learning groups. Within such groups children become more engaged with course material and, in the process of explaining it to one another, "respond differently than if they were only reading and listening" (Roger Johnson in Brandt, 1987, 17). Furthermore, they suggest that as our educational system has demanded that students master complex material more quickly, it has become essential that children be provided with the social support required to deal successfully with this added pressure. "The point is that the ability to cope is determined not by the amount of stress a person is under, but by the balance between the stress and the support. And much of that support has to come from peers" (David Johnson, in Brandt, 1987, 17).

Concerned about the highly individualistic tendencies encountered in American schools, Bronfenbrenner and Cagan have sought to identify educational strategies aimed at developing in children a sense of collective responsibility. They have turned to educational practices in socialist countries to find examples of such strategies. Of particular interest to Bronfenbrenner has been the use of cross-age tutoring as a means for nurturing a recognition of social obligation. He describes, for example, the practice of *shevstvo*, in which a class of older students adopts a younger,

> with each younger child having an older "brother" or "sister" from the more advanced class. It becomes the responsibility of the older pupil to get to know his younger "sib" and his family, to escort him to and from school, play with him and his friends, teach him games, and last, but not least, become acquainted with his progress and problems in school, reading with and to him, helping and encouraging him to learn. In the meantime the parent class as a whole organizes activities for their "ward class," including trips to athletic events, nature walks, campouts, museum visits, etc. (1970, 157)

Such experiences reinforce the recognition of interdependence for both younger and older children.

Like Noddings, Bronfenbrenner argues that children should be given ways to contribute to the well-being of the entire educational community. He describes educational offerings in Russian schools that provide children with the opportunity to care for class gardens and obtain training in "skills like carpentry, metal work, automotive mechanics, dressmaking, radio repair, computer programming, and the building of scale models for science and industry" (Bronfenbrenner, 1970, 49). Students are also given responsibility for dealing with discipline problems that arise among their peers (Bronfenbrenner, 1970, 63–69). Drawing upon the Russian experience, Bronfenbrenner argues that American students should be given responsible tasks both within the school and beyond it, in the larger community. Cagan believes that attempts by socialist educators to instill a cooperative and socially responsible ethic succeed to the extent they do because children are given the opportunity to actively live out the prosocial behaviors valued by their teachers and the broader society (1978, 259).

In her article "Community and Schools," educational philosopher Raywid (1988) suggests that schools may be one of the last sites in American society where children even have the possibility of experiencing what it means to be affiliated with others beyond the nuclear family. She argues that because schools are places where a sizable proportion of students remain with one another for a number of years, they possess two of the characteristics of functional communities: shared space and the opportunity to interact with others in a variety of ways (204). She notes that many alternative schools consciously take advantage of these factors and take steps to build a sense of community among their students and faculty. She further notes that if such schools are chosen by parents who share similar points of view, they could become the loci of community-building activities that extend beyond the boundary of the school itself. She acknowledges that there are dangers in such a project, the foremost of which are parochialism, the construction of undesirable forms of community, and the tendency in most communal situations to inhibit reflection about the process by which people are socialized to accept shared norms (205–07). She believes, however, that steps can be taken to address these dangers. Doing so may well be necessary if we hope to provide settings in which our human need to "commune and covenant" with others is satisfied. In her analysis, she points to the role educators could play in reconnecting children to the broader social environments in which they live and to the people with whom they interact within the school. Smaller schools of choice may provide one vehicle for reestablishing an educational process that reflects the needs and values of particular communities of families.

This brief review serves to demonstrate that a number of issues raised earlier have been topics of concern among educational thinkers. Although these concerns and the proposals that have arisen from them have been marginal to practices encountered in most American schools, they do offer additional guidance about steps which could be taken to reintegrate schools into the broader human communities of which they are a part. What is absent in nearly all these proposals, however, is a recognition that regenerating social forms based upon an experience of interdependence may become a necessity not simply because of social or psychological factors, but because of environmental developments that have only recently come to light. As a result, children may need to recognize not only their interrelatedness with one another, but also with elements of the natural environment in which their own human communities are located. Despite this limitation, the works of authors discussed in this section provide additional theoretical grounding, as well as practical strategies, that could contribute to the formulation of an educational process more suited to the requirements of a world in which economic progress and the individual opportunities predicated upon it are no longer guaranteed.

Conclusion

By strengthening the ties between school and the social and natural worlds around it, by grounding learning in personal experience rather than abstractions that have little to do with children's lives, and by creating opportunities for children to form mutually supportive relations with others within the school, educators could begin the process of helping their students master habits of care, social responsibility, and commitment to others. It is important to ask, however, why such an educational process, disregarded in many respects throughout the twentieth century, is any more likely to find favor now than in earlier decades.

This question raises the issue of whether the schools can in fact play any role in contributing to the transition from the now dominant modern/industrial worldview to the one that appears to be emerging in response to the environmental crisis. Whereas it has been common in the United States to turn to public education as the solution to a variety of social problems, contemporary scholarship has suggested that cultural institutions like the schools interact closely with economic and political institutions and are largely dependent upon the nature of these critical spheres of human activity. Though schools can serve as one site of social change, if comparable changes are not also enacted within the marketplace and government, educational experiments are likely to be short-lived and ineffectual (Apple, 1982; Carnoy and Levin, 1985; Williams, 1961). This is one of the reasons given for the limited impact of the progressive innovations sponsored by Dewey and others in the teens and 1920s, and then later in the 1960s and 1970s (Bowles and Gintis, 1976).

If the conditions that have supported the growth and development of modernity were to continue, it seems likely that little could be done to alter the educational processes established to induct the young into a competitive market society. Those conditions, however, will not remain the same, and in fact are beginning to change in ways that challenge the practice and policies of contemporary schools. In a sense, the task that now faces educators concerned about preparing children for a world very different from our own is not dissimilar to the task taken up by Whig reformers such as Horace Mann a century and a half ago. The original proponents of the common school were able to anticipate the educational requirements of an industrial as opposed to agricultural economy. The schools that arose from their efforts served to prepare children to participate in a new and revolutionary world. The common school was able to become the dominant model of education because the public at large grew to believe that its training and certificates were linked to the achievement of personal security. Although the common school's solutions have been imperfect and never fully implemented, its successful induction of more and more children into a radically different social and economic order led it to become an increasingly popular institution.

It is becoming more and more clear, however, that the progress common school reformers assumed to be limitless is bounded. In such a situation, the norms imparted by contemporary schools will become counterproductive. What will be required in the future will be the introduction of norms that foster a lived recognition of interdependence. The dilemma faced by educators concerned about such issues, however, is that there is as yet no widespread acknowledgment of this possibility. Although environmental awareness is on the rise and an increasing number of people are beginning to understand that there may be deep contradictions between continued economic growth and ecological stability, few have yet taken to heart the implications of this contradiction for their own lifestyles and aspirations. It will thus be difficult to build much support for the implementation of the educational model discussed in this chapter upon claims of its practical utility.

Despite the absence of a widespread understanding of the impact that environmental developments may have on our lives, there is at present a deep concern about more immediate educational and economic problems that is leading to calls for major structural and pedagogical reforms in schools. Although the motivation for such reforms has little to do with the concerns raised here, many of the suggested reforms parallel those outlined in this chapter. The concern that is leading to their invention and dissemination has arisen from four primary factors. The most prominent among them is the failure of American schools to reduce the dropout rate below the 25 percent level where it has remained for the previous two decades. Although the majority of dropouts are white, this problem has become especially severe among minority populations in U.S. cities, where the dropout rate frequently ranges from 50 to 80 percent (Wehlage et al., 1989).

A second factor contributing to this concern is the increasingly high social and individual costs associated with school dropout (Catterall, 1987; Green, 1980). Unlike earlier decades when students unable or unwilling to complete their educations could still gain access to blue collar jobs with wages sufficient to support a family, occupational opportunities available to high school dropouts now offer virtually no possibility of attaining economic security or independence (William T. Grant Foundation, 1988). Students who fail to complete, at minimum, a high-school education may become members of a permanent underclass.

A third factor is the likely possibility of a serious shortage of skilled labor in the 1990s, coupled to an increased proportion of elderly citizens dependent upon an expanding tax base for their support (Hodgkinson and Mirga, 1986; Johnston, 1987). If a significant number of students fail to master the increasingly sophisticated skills required to participate in our "postindustrial" labor market, the economic competitiveness of the United States could be threatened. Furthermore, the wage-scale of this group of poorly trained U.S. workers would be so low that the government could conceivably become unable to generate adequate resources to sustain the Social Security system. Although the knowledge and skills of the U.S. labor force must be seen as only one contributing factor to the viability of the U.S. economy, some corporate leaders are beginning to place pressure on schools to alter their practice in the direction of the reforms proposed here as a result of these possibilities (Committee for Economic Development, 1987).

Finally, projected demographic changes suggest that in the future more rather than fewer students will share background characteristics that have been associated with school failure (Hodgkinson, 1988). This will mean that unless action is taken now to address these problems, they will become more severe in the years ahead.

This combination of factors is resulting in increased attention to the educational needs of students, now commonly called children at risk, who in the past have been allowed to fail. As Hodgkinson (1988) notes, earlier in this century schools could act as a selection device, identifying, rewarding, and advancing students capable of making the most contribution to a continued expansion of the forces of production. He argues, however, that in our present circumstances, schools can no longer only identify the "winners"; they must now create winners if we hope to sustain the quality of our common life. Since the work of educators has been dominated by tasks of identifying and sorting children of varied talents, however, few conventional schools exemplify the structures, attitudes, or educational practices needed to actively improve the performance of initially weak students.

A small but growing number of programs, however, are taking on the task of educating children who otherwise are at risk of dropping out. Schools that achieve this end are often characterized by a set of behavioral and programmatic regularities that run counter to those which foster the transmission of the norms of detached independence and competitive achievement encountered in most conventional schools. The failure of at-risk students appears to be at least partially linked to their inability or unwillingness to adopt these norms. Educators concerned about their success have developed practices and strategies that are aimed at bringing children at risk of failure in from the margins of the school into an experience of membership, belonging, and commitment. In the process, they often replicate the social relations and forms of interaction and support encountered in well-functioning primary groups. Furthermore, in the more effective programs, they have developed instructional practices that encourage active participation rather than passive detachment.

In the next chapter, I demonstrate how many of the features of the educational model described here and proposed at different times throughout the twentieth century are in fact being adopted by teachers in such programs. In the concluding chapter I discuss strategies for encouraging the more widespread dissemination and adoption of such reforms on the premise that the development of special schools for the poor and the marginalized may provide at least one vehicle for introducing elements of the alternative worldview described earlier with its acknowledgment of embeddedness and the need for collective support and action.

Six

❂

Schools for At-Risk Youth: A Starting Point for Educational Change

As indicated in the conclusion of the preceding chapter, educators are discovering that for a number of reasons children at risk for academic failure respond positively to a school environment that actively attempts to draw them into the experience of social bonding and school membership, and that explicitly links learning activities to student interests and concerns (Foley and McConnaughy, 1982; Hamby, 1989; Hanh, Danzberger, and Lefkowitz, 1987; Wehlage et al., 1989). Why these strategies work is not fully understood, but two possible explanations are related to students' need for support and care.

For some students, schools may provide one of the few locations in which they have access to adult attention and concern (Bronfenbrenner, 1986; Coleman and Hoffer, 1987; Raywid, 1988). Those students reared in families in which contact with adults is either minimal or abusive may lack the self-esteem, confidence, or social skills required to negotiate the school's demands (Dreeben, 1968). Establishing quasi-familial relations with their teachers lays the foundation upon which further learning can be constructed (Wehlage et al., 1989).

For other students, the absence of such support in school may contrast with the more cooperative relations they encounter within their own homes and neighborhoods. This can become a source of personal dissonance or resistance (Connell et al., 1982; Gans, 1962; Goldstein, 1985; Weis, 1985). These students become unwilling to adopt the school's norms of detached independence and achievement because doing so may attenuate relations with others essential for their own security and well-being. Lacking the desire to adopt the school's definition of success, they often fail. By providing a social environment in which educational attainment is not linked to the abandonment of mutually supportive relations, alternative schools offer at-risk students the opportunity to earn a diploma, learn some of the knowledge and skills required to participate in the mainstream economy, and yet develop or maintain ties to their own families and communities.

In this chapter I describe educational practices encountered in four schools for students who are generally considered to be educationally at risk. Three of the schools—the Madison Memorial School-Within-a-School, Sierra Mountain High School, and the Media Academy—were associated with a national study of 14 promising programs for at-risk students conducted under the auspices of the National Center on Effective Secondary Schools at the University of Wisconsin-Madison. Findings from this study have been published in *Reducing the Risk: Schools as Communities of Support* (Wehlage et al., 1989). Research conducted during this study indicated that practices observed in these programs are representative of the kinds of innovative approaches now being developed nationwide to address the educational needs of students often marginalized in conventional schools.

The fourth school, St. Mary's on the Andreafsky, was not involved in the previous study, but is the subject of an ethnographic account by Judith Smilg Kleinfeld (1979). Serving a population of Alaskan Eskimo students, this school also works with children considered to be at risk of school failure. Unlike the three other programs and most alternative schools developed for marginal students, however, St. Mary's aims are more clearly directed toward integrating students into a social environment where mutual support and a recognition of interdependence with the natural world are more in evidence than they are in our own society. Regardless of St. Mary's more explicit articulation of an educational program aimed at engendering mutual support and an acknowledgment of interdependence, the structures, instructional practices, curriculum, and social relations encountered in this school are very similar to those found in successful programs for at-risk youth. Furthermore, Kleinfeld discovered that a sizable proportion of students who had graduated from St. Mary's exemplified the forms of social responsibility, commitment, and involvement that may be required of us all if economic conditions worsen significantly. St. Mary's offers some, though not decisive, evidence that the educational model presented in Chapter 5 may result in the adoption of social practices and attitudes that reflect a recognition of our attachment to other people and the natural world.

It is in their attempts to encourage student participation and retention that programs for at-risk children have much to teach educators in more conventional schools, and it is these attempts which could provide a vehicle for introducing forms of educational practice more likely to nurture attachment rather than the alienation experienced by a growing number of students. To encourage the development and implementation of the educational structures, processes, and content appropriate for a sustainable rather than an expanding economy, educators could expropriate current efforts to increase the achievement and retention of at-risk students, attempting to disseminate them to a broader range of schools. If such an educational process were additionally linked to collective activities related to local economic and community development, students would also be given the opportunity to apply lessons in cooperation learned within the school to the broader environment in which they live their lives. When and if the ecological and economic developments discussed in Chapter 1 begin to contribute to a reduction in the forces of production, educators could then make their own agenda regarding the teaching of both social and natural interdependence more explicit.

Madison Memorial School-Within-A-School[1] (Madison, Wisconsin)

The Madison Memorial School-Within-a-School was established in 1984 in an effort to reduce the dropout rate among students who were seriously deficient in credits by the time they reached their junior year in high school. The program is small, enrolling no more than 64 students divided more or less equally between the junior and senior classes. It is staffed by three full-time teachers who provide instruction in science, English, and social studies, and a half-time secretary. Six additional teachers from the larger high school in which the School-Within-a-School is located offer courses in math, physical education, and vocational subjects such as marketing, office skills, and food services. The School-Within-a-School is especially relevant to arguments raised here because of its success in creating a sense of common purpose and mutual support within the school and its efforts to link formerly alienated students to the broader community beyond the school.

One of the strongest elements of this program is its work experience program. A central concern of teachers in the School-Within-a-School is helping students master both the academic and social skills they will need to make a transition to employment once they have earned their diplomas. To assist with this transition, they have devised a series of vocational units scheduled during the afternoon that are required of all juniors. Three of these units take place outside the school for a nine-week period each. In one, a team of approximately 16 students works with a community organization that involves at-risk youth in housing renovation projects. In another, students are assigned to day-care centers. During the third vocational experience students work in different health-care institutions. In each case, juniors in the program are given the opportunity to work with adults outside the school on projects that have an obvious effect on the broader community.

The validation many of them receive from adults who appreciate their effort and labor can act as a powerful tool for reconnecting them to a sense of their own possibilities and for helping them recognize the valuable contributions they can make to others. The activities they engage in also demand active participation and can lead to a renewed belief in their own competencies. Students involved in carpentry tasks, for example, often take genuine pleasure in their acquisition of new skills and the completion of projects such as insulating an attic or installing drywall. Others can experience a similar sense of affirmation as a result of working with elderly people in a retirement home. After completing this experience, students during their senior year are required to find their own paid employment, for which they also receive credits required for graduation. These experiences likewise serve to reduce the boundary between the school and the community and are aimed at diminishing the alienation and disaffection that are often contributing factors to the academic failure of many of these students.

Within the academic component of the School-Within-a-School, steps are also taken to overcome the experience of marginality. It is not uncommon for students who enroll in this special program to have been outcasts of one sort or another—students who label themselves as "dirtballs" or "punkers," or students who have recently moved from another city and never found a group with whom they could connect. Many of the students in the School-Within-a-School are also from lower socioeconomic backgrounds. In a parent school that is primarily composed of middle- and upper middle-class students, this, too, contributes to their sense of being outsiders.

Teachers in the program attempt to overcome student alienation and provide support in a variety of ways. A classroom teacher/student ratio of 1:16 and students' two-year long participation in the program provide the structural conditions that allow for the formation of closer ties between adults and youth in the School-Within-a-School.

Teachers, furthermore, expect to interact with students in a more comprehensive manner than that generally encountered in most high schools. The head teacher of the program, for example, is involved in classroom instruction for only two periods a day. This means that during other classes he or she is able to meet with students who require more intensive counseling or to stand in for his colleagues who decide that counseling a particular student is more important than working with an entire class. Although some students feel that teachers in the School-Within-a-School "care too much," others appreciate their willingness to "talk about anything" and to become more than just academic specialists.

The fact that the School-Within-a-School is small and that classes are limited to no more than 16 students also facilitates the development of close ties among the youth enrolled in the program. Classes, furthermore, remain together as they move from one morning subject to another. Teachers do not rely simply upon student proximity to create a sense of affiliation and membership, however. They consciously offer activities such as school picnics, field trips, and an annual ropes/challenge course for entering juniors to engender social bonding. The ropes/challenge course, in particular, is viewed by students as being pivotal to their willingness to open up to other people in the program. After a day of trust exercises that culminate in falling backwards from a four-foot-high platform into the arms of their peers and teachers, helping one another over a log suspended ten feet from the ground, and seeing that everyone in their group scales a 14-foot-high wall, students report experiencing a new kind of relatedness with their classmates. As one girl reported:

> Before the [ropes course] you didn't really trust people with yourself. You'd trust them with maybe your ideas and stuff, but like in the stress course you had to trust people to lift you up and lift you over things and carry you places and hold on to you so that you didn't fall.... (in Smith, 1987a, 14)

Teachers refer back to the mutual support students have experienced in this contrived yet meaningful setting during weekly awards assemblies when students are also informed about peers who need

> everyone's help to deal with attendance or academic problems. They are reminded of the ropes course and told that they can assist one another with attendance and course work in the same way they boosted one another over logs. Such support does

occur. Students as well as the school secretary will call classmates who appear to be cutting. One friend will counsel another
if he or she is considering dropping or pointing out of the program. Students also responded positively when asked whether
they seek out and receive help from one another on class assignments. (Smith, 1987a, 15)

Although not all students in the program are drawn into this closer
sense of affiliation, enough are so that when asked to describe the
nature of social interaction in the program, many students compare it
to a family. As one boy who had earned enough credits to join the
senior class mid-year reported, "[W]hen I got moved up, it's like
everybody was happy for me, but they were kind of sad that I wasn't
in their class anymore. And that kind of made me feel good, too, just
knowing that we are all together" (in Wehlage et al., 1989, 22).

When the School-Within-a-School is compared to the educational model described in Chapter 5, however, three primary elements are
missing. The first is one that will be missing in the descriptions of the
next two programs as well: the establishment of a closer working relationship between teachers and students' families. There is a tendency
among teachers at the School-Within-a-School to view their students'
parents as deficient and incompetent. They believe that they must
take on the task of parenting themselves, because they assume their
students' parents have been unable or unwilling to fulfill this responsibility. As a result, they make few efforts to reach out to students'
families. When students are counseled, they are treated as individuals
detached from broader social relations. Parent conferences are rare at
the School-Within-a-School. This orientation is also reflected in teachers' acknowledgment that the program is aimed at modifying the
behavior of its students and resocializing them in ways deemed more
acceptable by the dominant society. Because their families have not
taught School-Within-a-School students to "get their acts together"
and "to function in society," their teachers believe that they themselves must. The opposition between school and home that has been a
consistent feature of American educational institutions since the mid-
1800s is thus perpetuated in this program.

The second element that is missing is related to the first and
involves the values that appear to be transmitted in this program.
Teachers in the School-Within-a-School are primarily concerned
about helping their students learn how to get along—in the school
and in the workplace. They want them to become responsible students and workers willing to observe social conventions of punctuali-

ty, personal neatness, reliability, trustworthiness, and tactfulness. Though such conventions in themselves are not undesirable, they are not geared toward the development of the forms of collective responsibility and action that may be required if material conditions are significantly altered.

Finally, in the School-Within-a-School's academic classes students tend to remain the passive recipients of an education developed and delivered by their teachers. Although group discussions are common, the incorporative educational model described in Chapter 3 remains dominant. Students are still expected primarily to absorb information presented by their teachers and reproduce it on worksheets or tests. The kinds of active and experiential learning that could lead to higher levels of educational engagement are not much in evidence in core academic subjects. Whereas such engagement is present during the vocational component of the School-Within-a-School, the conditions that might foster student involvement in the mastery of academic material required for postsecondary training have not been systematically developed.

Without minimizing the seriousness of these weaknesses, let us note that the School-Within-a-School does demonstrate a number of characteristics which have facilitated the reattachment of many of its students to the process of education, to their teachers, and to one another. The development of internship and employment opportunities in the broader community, as well as the program's creation of a more supportive and caring social environment, serves to overcome some of the experience of alienation and isolation that had been problematic for its students in the conventional high school. If these elements were combined with other elements of the model described in Chapter 5, the School-Within-a-School could conceivably draw even more of its students into the forms of social membership and support its teachers view as desirable.

Sierra Mountain High School (Grass Valley, California)

Sierra Mountain High School is an alternative program for ninth and tenth graders who had developed patterns of truancy and school failure. The school, founded in 1980, is staffed by a principal, eight teachers, an aide, three secretaries, and one maintenance man—all of whom interact in a variety of ways with the program's approximately 90 students. The high ratio of adults to students at this school is made possible by the operation of a second independent learning program for older students and adults in the late afternoon and evening. The school receives the same allocation of State funds for students in both programs.

Staff members at Sierra Mountain believe their most important tasks are to create an educational program capable of "hooking" students back into the process of education and to enhance their self-esteem. They seek to achieve these ends by developing classes that tend to provide many opportunities for active participation and a school climate which is personally embracing and supportive. Unlike the School-Within-a-School, which is housed within a parent high school, Sierra Mountain has its own facility located on 11 acres, two miles from the nearest town. Within this setting, teachers have taken the opportunity to develop a diverse and at times unusual array of classes as well as an informal and tolerant social environment.

Sierra Mountain offers a core curriculum of conventional academic subjects, supplemented with an appealing variety of elective courses. Among these are classes in guitar making, peer counseling, photography, computers, stitchery, gardening, musical composition on an electronic synthesizer, small building and log cabin construction, and school maintenance. This curriculum reveals a belief shared among staff at Sierra Mountain that students who have failed in school require classes that focus as much or more on experiential learning than on the forms of incorporative education encountered in most conventional classrooms.

A similar emphasis can be found in academic courses in which teachers strive to develop lessons that require participation rather than passivity. In English, for example, much time is spent reading plays or stories aloud and writing. And in science, efforts are made to take students into the field with some frequency. In addition to studying the pond located on the school's property, interested students can take trips to wilderness areas in the Sierra Nevada Range and on the Pacific Coast to supplement classroom activities. Although none of these courses specifically draws upon students' outside-of-school experiences, most provide opportunities to learn while doing. Instruction thus involves activities that are primarily concrete rather than abstract; furthermore, it allows students to acquire knowledge that is at least partly based upon their own explorations rather than the explorations of others. At Sierra Mountain, classwork generally demands participation rather than detached observations.

Educators at Sierra Mountain similarly seek to enhance students' self-esteem by drawing them into the school community, rather than allowing them to maintain the position of outsiders looking in. Many of the students at Sierra Mountain had experienced a significant degree of isolation and incongruence at the district's large comprehensive high schools. In contrast to what Sierra Mountain students considered to be an uncaring, unresponsive, and punitive environment at their former schools, many found staff and student relations at this alternative program to be supportive and embracing. Teachers, for example, are called by their first names. Staff members consciously adopt expanded roles and make themselves available as counselors, friends, or confidants. As one teacher observed,

> I tend to treat the kids with respect, and come straight across with them. I have expectations of what their behavior should be and what their achievement should be in my classes, and I put that out without any conditions to my respect other than respect returned. I think that I put out affection for these kids. I feel real protective of them. They're my kids. I think that helps. Treating the kids with a feeling that they are your kids, the kids sense that. They sense that I care about them and what happens to them. (in Smith, 1987b, 6)

Many students are highly responsive to this form of care and concern. As one student noted: "[I]f you need to talk about [something] they'll take you aside and they'll help you, whatever it is, whether it's school problems, problems in that class, or family problems" (in Smith, 1987b, 6). She further observed that teachers at Sierra Mountain are more approachable because "[T]hey seem like sisters and brothers as well as teachers" (in Smith, 1987b, 6).

Teachers also attempt to encourage students to become affiliated with the school by giving those who respond positively to its ethos and values the opportunity to assume responsibility for different elements of the program. Rather than seeing students as potential adversaries, teachers seek to form alliances and draw them into the life of the school. Two primary student activities involve running the school store and serving on the student court to which students can turn if they object to the punishment meted out to them by the principal or counselor for rule infractions such as cutting or showing disrespect to teachers or peers. The student court has the authority to assign whatever "sentence" (generally one to four hours of work around the school campus during "Saturday school") they believe is appropriate. Student participation and leadership are also cultivated in various club activities.

To some extent, Sierra Mountain's small size allows for the formation of closer bonds to peers. The formation of these bonds is encouraged by the school's ethos, with its focus on what are called the *four A's:* acceptance, appreciation, affection, and attention. Staff members attempt to model these qualities and transmit them to students. One student leader observed: "People are taught that [the 4 A's]. People here live by that" (Smith, 1987b, 5).

Instructional practices and teacher/student relations at Sierra Mountain demonstrate ways in which educators of at-risk youth can create engaging learning experiences and take steps to provide increased adult support and care for their students. In these ways, this program offers useful guidance about how elements of the model described in Chapter 5 can be given shape. During the year of our study, however, what was most missing from that model at Sierra Mountain was any serious attempt to integrate students' educational and social experiences into the broader community. Although teachers there had created a school that was culturally comfortable for a sizable share of their students, Sierra Mountain essentially operated as an island set apart both from the dominant community and the families of its students. Sierra Mountain offered the experience of social bonding, especially between students and teachers, within its narrow boundaries, but by and large that experience was not extended to others. Since our study, however, Sierra Mountain has taken steps to establish a "community-as-school" program that provides students with internship opportunities in local agencies and businesses. This program could help rectify some of the isolation and insularity that had earlier characterized the school.

The Media Academy (Oakland, California)

Perhaps because the Media Academy continually gives its students the opportunity to share their concerns in print or on local radio stations about school, city, national, and global concerns, the link established between this program and the broader community within which it is embedded is stronger than at either Sierra Mountain or the School-Within-a-School. Established in 1986 as a special program at Fremont High School in Oakland, the Media Academy was created by a group of four teachers, including the director of the school's award-winning journalism program, who were concerned about the lack of motivation and occupational direction among Fremont's predominantly African American, Latino, and Asian students. They wanted to find some way to demonstrate to these students the link between education and future vocational possibilities, as well as to involve them in a sequence of interrelated learning activities that would be intrinsically interesting and rewarding.

The program they created enrolls approximately 50 new sophomores each fall. Students are asked to make a three-year commitment to the Academy, although those who wish may return to the conventional high school. Few have done so. Once enrolled, sophomores are broken into two classes of approximately 25 students each. They generally attend journalism, English, social studies, biology, and mathematics classes together. Although this pattern is not continued during their junior and senior years, students will continue to take core journalism courses together, and many will choose to work with one another on the school's newspapers, *The Green and Gold* and *El Tigre* (a Spanish/English community paper), or the yearbook.

Pivotal to this program is the establishment of a multiplicity of ties to the broader community. Perhaps most important is the relationship teachers have built with representatives of local media establishments. On the Academy's Advisory Committee sit, among others, the editor and publisher of the *Oakland Tribune*, the director of Pacific News Service, the director of the journalism institute at University of California-Berkeley, and representatives from a number of radio and television stations. This committee provides the Academy with both curricular and financial support (Wehlage, 1987, 10). Curricular support takes a number of forms. One of the most significant is the participation of media professionals in the teaching of journalism courses. A reporter, for example, might make a presentation about following leads and developing a story. Efforts are made to invite media representatives who share similar backgrounds to Academy students or who grew up in the same neighborhoods. Members of the Advisory Committee also provide students with opportunities to air their written work on radio, as well as offer summer internships during which Academy students are able to get firsthand experience working in a media operation. Field trips to newspapers, an international telecommunications center, and radio and television stations are a regular part of the Academy program. In these ways, students learn about the media profession in the same way that an Eskimo child learns about hunting or fishing: by watching and talking with adults who are practicing this trade. At the Media Academy, the boundary between school and community has become permeable.

Learning about the trade, however, is not simply a matter of watching and listening. Students are given many opportunities to practice what they have observed and heard. As at Sierra Mountain, teachers at the Media Academy present lessons that encourage if not demand involvement. This involvement is particularly in evidence when Academy students work on the school's publications. As reported by Wehlage (1987),

> Every day the Media Academy complex is a constant rush of activity. Students move in and out depending on their schedules and the tasks they are pursuing. Cameras are checked out, the dark room door opens and closes, notebooks are retrieved, plans for the next issue of the paper are discussed, stories are typed and friends are met for socializing. (12)

Students on the publication staffs are given broad responsibility regarding topics for articles and editorials and are encouraged to write about issues that are of immediate concern to themselves and the broader community. Editorials or news reports on topics such as date rape, reverse discrimination, drug abuse, or abortion are commonly found in the program's publications. Students are further expected to assume significant authority in overseeing the completion of necessary tasks. In many respects, the Academy's papers belong to the students; teachers in the program give them the assistance they need to do the best job possible. At the Media Academy, then, students are inducted into an occupational field through participation in a variety of concrete activities that lead to socially valued products.

More than connections to the community and a course of study that demands participation characterize the Media Academy, however. Also in evidence in this program is a sustained attempt on the part of teachers to cultivate a more supportive and interdependent social environment. Although teachers' relationships with students are to some extent more professional and less "therapeutic" than those encountered at the School-Within-a-School and Sierra Mountain, the coaching, mentoring, and advocacy they offer students leads to a comparable experience of closeness and attachment. This can be very important for students who may never have had such a relationship with a teacher. One boy who did particularly well at the Academy spoke of the impact that this kind of care had on his own attitude toward school. "I had never experienced this before where the teachers are close and encourage me. I was just a C+/B- student, but now I am an A/B student" (in Wehlage, 1987, 19).

Because they are able to work with the same students over a three-year period, teachers are given the opportunity to observe student growth in ways generally inaccessible to most educators. This gives them the chance to cultivate student abilities in a more developmental, rather than directive fashion. Students are encouraged to take responsibility and cultivate their own competencies within a teaching and learning environment that is committed to their success and to the discovery of what the lead teacher at the Media Academy calls the "gold" that exists in each student. Furthermore, the development of those competencies is aimed at something more than just personal fulfillment; it is linked to the growing contribution students can make to the collective work of the Academy itself.

Involvement in these shared tasks has nurtured the evolution of supportive social relations among students as well. By and large, students are able to work with the same team of peers for a three-year period. This gives them a chance to get to know one another with a degree of intimacy generally not possible in most school environments. One student noted, for example, that "[W]hen you're a sophomore you feel unsure of yourself around all the new students. By staying together students get to know each other more quickly and the adjustment to high school is easier" (in Wehlage, 1987, 16). The interaction of older and more experienced students with their younger colleagues in the Academy is also important. In the production room, in particular, incoming students have the opportunity to observe older students demonstrating the skills they are learning in their courses. As Wehlage reports, "The sophomores can see the responsibility that exists for the production of the paper and yearbook. The fledgling journalists can experience, sometimes vicariously, the process that is occurring" (1987, 14). Wehlage further observes that the cohort education in evidence at the Media Academy provides a setting in which students come to feel that they are members of a community engaged in a common task. "The image of collective success increases the likelihood of individual success. This can serve to reinforce positive views of self and the future. It can help sustain the weak in the face of adversity" (1987, 28). Perhaps because of this support, students no longer condemn the academic success of their peers. As one girl observed, "No one is put down for doing well in subjects" (in Wehlage, 1987, 21). In this program, individual achievement takes on collective meaning and is not something that divides students from one another.

Despite the Media Academy's close ties to the broader community and its ability to engender a sense of affiliation among the students and adults who participate in the program, one of the primary aims of the Academy remains helping its students gain the skills and attitudes required to break away from their own neighborhoods and backgrounds. Teachers at the Media Academy, like those at the School-Within-a-School and Sierra Mountain, tend to see the home life of their students as debilitating, if not destructive. They view themselves as potential bridges to a lifestyle that promises more opportunities for their students. As one instructor in the program said, "This is God's work that we are engaged in. We can not become discouraged; we are the last line of defense protecting them from disaster" (in Wehlage, 1987, 24). This teacher went on to note that "Fifty percent of the kids face problems that are due to their parents. Parents neglect their children, don't know how to help them acquire the skills they need in life, and create pathological home environments" (25). Instead of helping parents gain those skills—something that educators associated with James Comer's efforts in New Haven elementary schools have successfully accomplished (Comer 1988)—teachers in the Media Academy tend to draw their students into a new and more appealing community that stands to some degree in opposition to the life they know in their own neighborhoods. Again, this orientation can lead to the attenuation of ties to family members seen as inadequate by teachers whose orientation is more clearly middle class.

Although it must be admitted that the social pathologies observed by teachers in the Media Academy do exist, if the employment opportunities for which they are now preparing their students become less available, it will become increasingly difficult for students to leave their families and friends in hope of becoming independent media professionals. The temporary community they will have experienced at the Media Academy will then have done nothing more than divorce them from their original primary groups; after high school, there may be no similar community to which its graduates will be able to turn. Another approach that educators in this program might take would be to develop instructional strategies aimed not at liberating children from "the accident of birth," but at helping them to use that accident to good ends. For example, instead of seeing the development of competency as a means for helping students escape from the social disaster of the Oakland ghetto, educators might consciously direct their students' attention back to that ghetto, not simply as a subject for journalistic exploration, but as the "project" to which they could address their adult careers. Utilizing the cooperative skills and sense of personal potential cultivated during their years at the Media Academy, they could pool their talents and energies in an effort to regenerate their own families and neighborhoods and deal with larger political and economic practices that have contributed to their poverty. As the kind of escape for which the Media Academy is preparing its students becomes the prerogative of the few, the social welfare of the many may depend upon the willingness of increasingly more people to do just this.

St. Mary's on the Andreafsky (Near Bethel, Alaska)

It may only be as economic conditions worsen for members of the middle class that educators will begin thinking seriously of adopting such strategies. At that point, they may see that many of the pathological behaviors associated with poverty have less to do with individual character than with the social and economic health of communities. Given this understanding, the task of programs for at-risk youth would then become the revitalization of those communities, rather than the extraction of a few lucky individuals from them. Few schools are even beginning to see their work in this light. One that has is a small Catholic boarding school located in western Alaska.[2] It demonstrates many of the elements of the model described in Chapter 5 and furthermore has been notably successful in preparing its students to take on significant leadership roles within their own communities after graduating from high school or university. Education at St. Mary's is not aimed at facilitating personal mobility, but at the mastery of skills required to fulfill important social responsibilities to one's own people (Kleinfeld, 1979, 115). Although this program does not deal specifically with the broader ecological events that could curtail the continued expansion of the forces of production, it is set within an environmental context where people have historically had no choice but to acknowledge natural limits.

Kleinfeld (1979), whose ethnographic account of St. Mary's forms the basis of the following description, became attracted to the school as a result of its graduates. Students who had attended St. Mary's and then gone on to the University of Alaska-Fairbanks were significantly more successful in completing a college education than Eskimo students who had attended comparable publicly supported boarding schools. Although St. Mary's students generally scored at approximately the same level on entrance examinations as their peers from other schools, they displayed a level of self-confidence, verbal ability, and psychic well-being that distinguished them from other Eskimo students. They exhibited what their professors came to call the "St. Mary's effect."

Kleinfeld notes that St. Mary's success in working with a population of students who have generally failed in mainstream schools is tied to the way in which educators at this Catholic school were able to fuse the dominant culture with the local Eskimo culture. This fusion occurred within the school's curriculum, values, and social relations. Although the school offered no specific bilingual, bicultural, or even vocational classes, elements of the students' traditions were integrated across all subjects. This was particularly true in courses such as homemaking and art, but also occurred in academic classes as well. A senior social studies class, for example, dealt with aboriginal culture and government, modern government, geography, and the Alaska Native Claims Settlement Act of 1971 (Kleinfeld, 1979, 76). This latter class was viewed as highly significant for students' future involvement in their own villages, and teachers took great care to make sure that students understood issues related to land selection and management.

In one class observed by Kleinfeld, the teacher introduced a game students could use to learn how to rate a parcel of land according to different categories such as mineral potential, gravel, and availability of fish and game. He then went on to explain how to make a color-coded land-use map for their villages. He stressed the importance of this lesson when he said to his students,

> To me this class will only be halfway successful. I take that back. It won't even be halfway successful. It won't be successful at all if you take this information and never do anything with it, if you go home and never open your mouth at a meeting and explain some of the things you could explain. The value of this is that you can take the information and share it with people. (in Kleinfeld, 1979, 77-78)

Students in this class were being exposed to exactly the kind of planning that people on the local level may need to enter into if we hope to exercise the forms of decentralized land stewardship required to avert environmental catastrophe. Because the Alaska Native Claims Settlement Act gives regional and village corporations significant authority over their own economic development, students knew that the knowledge and skills acquired in this class could be translated into action upon returning to their own communities.

Not only did the school teach skills that would be acknowledged as valuable by students' families and neighbors, it presented this instrumental knowledge within a framework of values similar to those most students had grown up with at home. Rooted in a Catholic belief in the importance of generosity, self-sacrifice, and perseverance, these values were compatible with the cultural ideals of traditional Eskimo society. Neither cultural setting supported the forms of individualistic achievement encountered in modern/industrial society and the schools that support it. Although Eskimo families did not participate in the governance of St. Mary's, they knew that the school was pursuing their own values and goals. As Kleinfeld writes, "The configuration of educational influences on St. Mary's students—home, school, and church—were pervasive, consistent, and mutually reinforcing" (1979, 133). The primary aim of its teachers was the formation among their students of a set of core values that would orient them throughout their adult lives. Rather than being at variance with the values they learned as children, as was generally the case in most other schools set up to educate Native Alaskan or Native American students (Collier, 1973; Wax, Wax, and Dumont, 1964), the school's values were simply an extension and refinement of those early lessons.

Moral instruction at St. Mary's gained its power because of the way in which the school presented children with an arena within which they could live out the generosity, commitment, and responsibility to others seen as important both at home and at school. Social relations between students and adults and among students at St. Mary's exemplified the forms of mutual aid found in communities where such support is a requirement of survival. St. Mary's essentially functioned as a small community in which students were encouraged to form close interpersonal ties with one another and their teachers. Over time, such ties became an expected part of the school environment, and students would demand that teachers make themselves available as friends and confidants. A majority of the teachers at St. Mary's were volunteers from out-of-state who would remain in residence at the school for one to four years. Young college graduates, they had few other responsibilities that interfered with their acceptance of such an expanded role. Most presented themselves as "whole people" rather than subject-matter instructors and treated their students in the same way. The school's highly personalized social environment was in fact very similar to the villages from which most students had come. Kleinfeld observes that

> People knew each other in many roles and across many situations. A volunteer and a young man at St. Mary's might be a teacher and student, coach and basketball player, comembers of a school repair crew, and buddies in late night bull sessions. (1979, 131)

Social control in the school was achieved largely through the maintenance of these relations and the power of group opinion. This, too, was similar to the nature of social control in most Eskimo villages.

Staff members at St. Mary's not only attempted to provide ongoing support for their students, they urged their students to provide such support for one another. Emphasis was placed on seeing oneself as a member of the entire school community, and teachers strove to diminish the importance of village groups, exclusive pairs of friends, and student romances in an effort to build a strong sense of group unity. As Kleinfeld reports, "Over and over students were told it was good to get to know other people and be friendly with everyone. This was a sign of growing up" (124). She includes an excerpt from a school editorial that deals with this issue:

> It is not easy to move out toward others whom you don't know so well. It takes courage, both to go out to others and to do something your own group might not approve of. The thing that makes it hard is mistrust. If you don't know people from one village very well, you may find it hard to trust them not to do something that may hurt you. The only thing that will overcome lack of trust, and the fear that goes with it, is getting to know others as people first, and not as things. We should think of others as human beings and accept them if only for that reason, which will then become more important than whether or not they belong to your group, or any other group or category. (124)

Older students, as well, played an important role in drawing incoming students into this ethos, though not necessarily through direct instruction. Kleinfeld notes that the influence of older peers took place spontaneously as younger students attempted to be accepted by imitating their behavior (1979, 121). Teachers also made it clear to older students that they had an obligation to set an example. One senior explained to Kleinfeld:

> Being a senior everyone looks up to you. You must set an example. It's sort of hard. All these things I feel responsible for. Like I'm secretary of the student council, representative of the student body at faculty meetings, chairman of the Liturgy Club, in charge of making posters. Also, being a senior and having to carry eight subjects. It's not easy. (1979, 121)

This student demonstrates the way in which St. Mary's encouraged the development of a personal identity linked to group membership and the obligations that accrued from it. In a fundamental way, the social environment at St. Mary's encouraged students to accept roles based upon their position within the school, rather than upon factors tied to individual achievement or specific personal talents. As Kleinfeld notes, students at St. Mary's were seen as individuals embedded in groups, rather than as collections of individuals, as tended to be the case in the public boarding schools with which she was also familiar (123). The sense of obligation expressed by the student just quoted, however, did not arise spontaneously. It was consciously cultivated by the school's staff from early on in a student's residence at St. Mary's.

The school's spoken emphasis on the importance of offering one's talents and energies back to the group was given practical form through the responsibility placed upon students to arrange their own social activities. Each class, for example, took turns planning Friday activities for the school as a whole. Failure to develop imaginative and entertaining activities was seen as letting down the entire school. Dorm roommates were responsible for planning activities within their dormitory section for Saturday nights. As a result of the regular demand to organize such events, students mastered a planning process that included the listing of alternatives, discussion of their feasibility, the development of consensus, the division of the goal into subtasks, and the assignment of subtasks to individuals or small groups (1979, 69).

This concrete expression of collective responsibility carried over into the out-of-school lives of St. Mary's graduates. Eighty percent of the school's graduates returned to their local communities, where many became informal leaders on school boards, the village council, or the health board. A survey of St. Mary's graduates from 1963 to 1970 revealed that 61 percent participated in unpaid civic activities. Twenty-five percent of these graduates participated in three or more activities (1979, 8). In a survey of Eskimo graduates of two public high schools, Kleinfeld found that such civic participation was much less common: "[O]nly 8 percent of the 26 graduates from 1970 and 1971 participated in civic affairs, compared to 48 percent of the 27 St. Mary's graduates" (1979, 9). Drawing from a follow-up survey of St. Mary's graduates, Kleinfeld includes the following responses as typical of their community involvement:

I am presently on the City Council and head the finance committee and various others. I am also on the Board of Directors for AVEC [Alaska Village Electrical Cooperatives] departments. I helped start a young people's organization in 1980 and served for one year. (1960s graduate)

Now I am on the Parent Advisory Committee, Head Start, village corporation board member, city council member. I have been on the school board and a member of the women's club. (1960s graduate)

I am now trying to start an association for village young people, carnival, Boy Scout's scoutmaster, set up a teen center. I would like to organize a region-wide youth organization. (1970s graduate) (1979, 8–9)

Such activities are at least partial indicators of the success the educational model found at St. Mary's has had on the development of a lived recognition of interdependence and social responsibility. Schooled in an environment in which they were reminded continuously of their broader obligations to others, a sizable proportion of St. Mary's graduates return to their home communities prepared to fulfill those obligations rather than seek their own economic mobility elsewhere.

It must be noted in closing that engendering the civic responsibility demonstrated by St. Mary's graduates was undoubtedly facilitated by their having spent their early childhoods in traditional communities where the social practice of mutual support had not yet been completely eroded by the forces of modernization. It was not necessary for teachers at St. Mary's to instill among their students a new set of core values that emphasized the importance of generosity and self-sacrifice. By and large, St. Mary's students had already been socialized to share such values. In our own society, an individualistic orientation has become significantly more widespread. Still, a cooperative ethic is not entirely absent among students from economically marginalized populations. Steinetz and Solomon (1986), for example, describe successful students from a working-class neighborhood in Boston who, after earning college degrees, returned to their home community to set up businesses in which they employed their childhood friends. Although such examples are uncommon, the loyalty to place and people they represent has not been eradicated from our society. The task of educators will be to seek out, support, and cultivate this experience of affiliation and collective responsibility and to use it as the foundation upon which the educational enterprise is itself constructed.

Conclusion

The difficulty of utilizing programs for at-risk youth as models or seedbeds for the kinds of educational reform that have concerned me here should not be underestimated. As indicated throughout this chapter, the motivating force behind the formation of such schools is not the restoration of a more broadly experienced sense of communal obligation as seen at St. Mary's on the Andreafsky. Rather, alternative programs are generally directed toward inducting into the dominant culture students who, for a variety of reasons, have fallen to the margins of conventional schools. The social vision shared by the staff at St. Mary's is not common among most educators, and developing it will not be easy. Regardless of this fact, teachers in many programs for at-risk students are altering traditional behavioral and programmatic regularities in ways that might further the dissemination of the hidden curriculum of an institution like St. Mary's. It remains questionable, however, whether such a curriculum, if unarticulated, will indeed lead to the forms of broader social membership and commitment I see as essential. It can also be argued that without the validation of such membership and commitment in the realms of economic and political activity, efforts by educators will go no further than the school door, if that far.

I have no clear response to these objections, other than the one raised at the conclusion of Chapter 5. To restate that argument briefly, as material conditions change, children will need to learn new relational patterns, both with one another and with the natural environment, if they hope to achieve satisfactory levels of personal security. If some institution can successfully help them adopt attitudes and behaviors that contribute to this end, that institution may win the allegiance of students and their parents. Although the numbers of teachers able or willing to articulate the vision of interdependence outlined here may initially be small, their ability to help children create decent lives for themselves could win the attention and support of other educators and parents. In this way, the values underlying the structures that are currently being developed in programs for at-risk youth could be reinforced more overtly.

Second, if employment opportunities become more restricted or if the number of working poor increases, more citizens will be required to adopt economic practices characteristic of nonmarket societies in order to maintain a modicum of personal and collective security. Although dominant economic and political institutions may not reflect social norms built upon a recognition of interdependence, the evolution of an alternative economy based upon shared resources and collective entrepreneurialism would require them. An educational process that furthered cooperation and commitment to the common good could prepare children for such alternative institutions. For such a model to become widespread, however, the general public will have to accept the possibility that the forms of individual mobility and security that have characterized our own era could become a thing of the past. Though this may require a cultural revolution of immense magnitude, such a revolution could become unavoidable if the predicted environmental events outlined in Chapter 1 in fact transpire.

In preparation for this increasingly likely development, it seems prudent to explore whatever means we have at our disposal to introduce an educational process capable of instilling in children the values and social practices required to live humanely in such a world. Making use of programs adapted to the needs of already economically disadvantaged populations is one of these means. We can hope for many others as well. Although programs such as the School-Within-a-School, Sierra Mountain, and the Media Academy will require significant modification before they become able to accomplish the ends set out here, they display many more of the characteristics of an education likely to lead to a recognition of social and environmental interdependence than those encountered in most conventional schools. These characteristics offer a shell within which the values of a more ecologically sensitive and mutually supportive culture might be transmitted. Given the fact that our society is not ready to accept the implications of the environmental crisis for our way of life, the dissemination of such shells could provide at minimum a way to put in place an educational process that from this vantage point appears to be more suited to the demands of the future. In the concluding chapter I will address steps that might be taken to facilitate the introduction of more programs like the ones described here.

Seven

❂

Strategies for Developing Schools for Sustainability and Mutual Support

The process by which educational models evolve or are transformed is poorly understood. Efforts on the part of educational researchers and activists over the past half century to alter the basic configuration of American schools have in nearly all respects been thwarted by an institutional culture that seems impermeable to fundamental change (Combs, 1988; Fullan, 1982; Sarason, 1982, 1990). This has not led to a halt in such efforts, but it has led policy analysts to become much more circumspect about the possibilities of social and educational engineering (Elmore, 1983). Human institutions are simply not malleable in the way that some inanimate substances are. This does not mean that they are unmalleable, for the means by which culture is transmitted and the forms of behavior required to participate successfully in adult society have in fact changed dramatically during the previous four centuries.

This transformation, however, has rarely been the result of planned interventions. It has instead been part of a broad evolution of multiple institutions that have interacted with one another in ways that have furthered growth in some directions and inhibited it in others. During the modern era, that growth has tended to nourish attitudes and behaviors associated with the belief that we can detach ourselves from the social and natural communities that surround us. It is these attitudes and behaviors that now appear to be so problematic. If our civilization is to survive the grave ecological and social consequences of this mistaken view, our institutions will have to evolve in another direction. The possible nature of that direction was discussed in Chapter 4. Our task as concerned citizens and educators may be to hold that direction in mind and encourage the development of school practices that support it, at least in part.

As indicated in the previous chapter, programs now being created for children at risk of school failure possess a number of characteristics that encourage the experience of social membership and attachment. Although these programs primarily utilize their social environments as a means for integrating alienated students back into the experience of schooling, rather than as a vehicle for regenerating communal structures within the broader society, they still may provide the ground in which the educational model described in Chapter 5 could take root. With this strategy in mind, it seems important to determine how such programs could be implemented more broadly. In the remainder of this chapter I spell out a strategy for developing constituencies of support among three populations that play a significant role in determining the direction of public education: policymakers, parents and students, and educators. Such support is in fact becoming evident in a variety of quarters right now.

Gaining the Support of Policymakers

By and large, policymakers at the state or national level cannot be counted upon to align themselves with a worldview that points to the necessity of relinquishing our faith in material progress, economic development, and the pursuit of individual self-interest. That faith, however, is being challenged by social developments that call into question the forms of possessive individualism that now dominate our society. In order to assure the education of students who in the past could be neglected because of the availability of blue-collar jobs that did not require academic skills, a number of national organizations including the Committee on Economic Development, the Council of Chief State School Officers, Public/Private Ventures, and the Carnegie Foundation for the Advancement of Teaching have proposed major reforms in the nature of public education aimed at increasing the degree of school membership and participation by children at risk of educational failure. All four organizations comment on the importance of establishing small, supportive educational communities for these students as a means for overcoming their estrangement and disengagement from school.

The Committee for Economic Development (1987), an independent research and educational organization composed of more than 200 business executives and educators representing a number of major U.S. corporations and universities, criticizes the factory-style design of most large contemporary schools, suggesting that this model is no longer appropriate for the development of the problem-solving and social skills needed by the United States in a postindustri-al economy.

> The large size of most urban schools, a compartmentalized approach to learning, and the low expectations of students by staff and administration often make it impossible to provide the sense of belonging and continuity that children from disadvan-taged homes—indeed, all children—need in order to prosper. (39-40)

To overcome this sense of isolation, especially at the middle school level, the authors of this report argue for the creation of smaller edu-cational clusters in which students can work with the same group of teachers and students for a longer period of time (1987, 56–57). At the high school level, they suggest that more alternative schools need to be provided to reduce the alienation of low achievers and increase their opportunity to interact with counselors and mentors (1987, 57).

In its report, *Elements of a Model State Statute to Provide Educational Entitlements for At-Risk Students*, the Council of Chief State School Offi-cers (1987) lists a number of promising practices encountered in pro-grams for educationally disadvantaged students that it feels should be implemented more widely. Some of these practices include reducing student-teacher ratios, using evaluative measures based upon mastery rather than comparisons with class or national norms, and the adop-tion of cooperative learning strategies and peer tutoring (10–11).

In *State Governments and At-Risk Youth: The Critical Link*, Richard H. deLone (1987) argues for Public/Private Ventures that successful programs for this population should include small classes that offer students the opportunity to learn in a supportive educational commu-nity where they will be treated as valued individuals (15).

Writing for the Carnegie Foundation, Gene Maeroff (1988) sug-gests that creating urban schools where students can experience a sense of belonging may be one of the most important strategies to be pursued in an effort to increase educational attainment and retention among at-risk students.

> Overcoming anonymity—creating a setting in which every stu-dent is known personally by an adult—is one of the most com-pelling obligations urban schools confront. Young people who

have few constructive relationships with adults need a sense of belonging. They need positive encounters with older people who serve as mentors and role models for both educational and social growth. Building community must be a top priority if students in urban schools are to academically and socially succeed. (24)

In each of these instances, emphasis is placed on the importance of recognizing the role of the social environment as an aid or hindrance to educational achievement. The belief that individuals can succeed as social atoms with little reliance upon others is not in evidence in these proposals. These organizations also speak of the need for schools to establish closer working relationships with parents and to develop forms of governance that allow teachers and building administrators to make fundamental decisions about the shape of their own educational programs. Although such proposals are countered by others such as David Kearns, former CEO of Xerox and now Deputy Secretary of Education in the Bush administration and Denis Doyle, Senior Research Fellow at the Hudson Institute (1988), who continue to be more concerned about standardization and competition than supportive social relations, they demonstrate the willingness of influential policymakers in the United States to consider the development of schools more likely to engender caring and cooperative forms of behavior. Though their reason for doing so remains tied to the general principles of the modern/industrial worldview, this does not mean that the social skills learned by children in such schools could not be turned to students' collective advantage.

Carnoy and Levin (1985) point out that changes in the workplace are also leading economic and political leaders to reevaluate the nature of learning encountered in most American classrooms. Whereas in the past mastery of basic literacy and numeracy, as well as the adoption of habits of behavior conveyed by the hidden curriculum were sufficient prerequisites for the majority of jobs on the U.S. labor market, in our own period workers are now required to possess a variety of analytical and social skills that the previous educational model is ill-suited to transmit. As more jobs demand increased levels of teamwork, problem solving, and initiative, Carnoy and Levin suggest that educators will encounter demands to alter their practice in ways that will give students training in group problem solving. Such lessons are likely to enhance student involvement and participation and diminish the abstract and individualistic forms of instruction so typical of American schools. Carnoy and Levin further believe that these reforms could contribute to expectations on the part of workers that they will be involved in fundamental decision making in their place of employment. In this way, developments in both the school and the workplace could contribute to the evolution of the forms of localized economic decision making and participation that could become necessary as reduced production and mobility demand more self-reliance and cooperation on the part of regional populations.

Changes in the nature of America's place in the international economic community are also leading to calls for the development of educational programs that focus on an awareness of global as well as national trends. Interestingly, current activities of some American corporations, with their emphasis on decentralization and local management as a means for enhancing participation in a global market, are not dissimilar to calls by environmentally oriented activists to think globally but act locally. Although mainstream educational spokespeople such as Ernest Boyer of the Carnegie Foundation rarely acknowledge the environmental reasons for cultivating such an orientation, their suggestions that we entertain curricular programs aimed at developing an "intellectual understanding of the new global agenda" (in Fiske, 1989, 18) could contribute to the broader perspective called for if we hope to respond adequately to the complex ecological systems in which we live.

In a number of ways, then, there is a perceptible movement among some policymaking groups in the United States toward educational reforms likely to increase students' sense of connectedness to one another and the broader environment. This movement is still not widespread, however, and for it to become a force in American education will require convincing a broader population of policymakers of the need to sponsor a fundamental reorientation of our schools. Doing so will entail demonstrating to them that schools which set learning within a challenging yet supportive environment can lead to higher rates of retention and increased student participation. As Andrew Hanh (1987) has reported, we now know what the characteristics of successful programs for at-risk children are; our task is to develop more schools that incorporate them.[1] The Committee on Economic Development, the Council of Chief State School Officers, Private/Public Ventures, and the Carnegie Foundation for the Advancement of Teaching all are working to some extent toward achieving this end. Although not all policymakers or corporate leaders would necessarily agree with the position taken by these groups, the fact that such proposals are being disseminated as widely as they are at minimum provides the possibility of vigorous debate regarding these issues.

Enlisting the Support of the General Public

As indicated earlier, public faith in the ability of state-supported schools to prepare children for adult society has waned significantly over the past decade. The authority, good intentions, and expertise of the majority of teachers—generally unquestioned by all but a handful of critics in earlier decades—has become the subject of ongoing debate in the media and in communities throughout the United States. The credibility of public education has been undermined. For this reason, schools may become much more amenable to institutional transformation than in the past.

This new depth of public discontent may be enough to prevent schools from absorbing and then diluting innovative practices, the strategy some scholars have suggested that schools have adopted to resist fundamental change throughout most of the twentieth century. Meyer and Rowan (1983), for example, argue that conventional educators did not need to modify their practice in substantial ways because the purpose of schools was not so much the successful education of all students as the bestowing of credentials essential for participation in a modern/industrial economy.

At present, however, the globalization of the world economy is demonstrating that the educational tender of the United States is not equivalent to that encountered in other countries and that schools whose overriding obligation is to discover which students can do the assignments and which cannot (Schlechty, 1989) are no longer sufficient. This has led both the general public and corporate leaders to examine more carefully the content and structure of schooling.

The widespread development of magnet schools or schools of choice is indicative of increased interest on the part of parents and students in different approaches to curriculum and pedagogy as well as school structure. No longer are the conventional elementary school or comprehensive high school accepted as the only or best model of education. As Sarason (1982) might say, the public has become willing to consider a broader universe of alternatives. Aware now of other possible educational models, a growing number of parents are unwilling to accept the forms of schooling they knew as children and are placing pressure on their districts to develop schools with a variety of different curricular or pedagogical foci. Although this movement has tended to benefit children from middle- and upper middle-class families most (Moore and Davenport, 1988), its linkage to desegregation efforts has meant that some children from economically disadvantaged homes have been able to take advantage of this reform. The development of specialized programs such as the Media Academy in Oakland, for example, must be seen as part of this larger reform movement aimed at the creation of schools of choice.

Though parental motivation for choosing such programs is often tied more to educational and economic competition than to a concern about social support and cooperation, many magnet schools or schools of choice are smaller and more focused than most comprehensive high schools (Blank, 1987 1989). They also attract faculty who often demand more participation in school governance and program development. Finally, they tend to function more as self-contained educational communities than simply one stage in a long and generally impersonal educational procession (Lipsitz, 1984; Metz, 1986; Raywid, 1988; Schofield, 1982). Their success and attractiveness may at least in part be linked to these characteristics, which are similar to the educational model described in the previous chapter. Again, the task for educators concerned about encouraging the development of schools capable of inducting children into a society where cooperation and collective support may be essential for human welfare will be to work with forms of educational experimentation that are already the object of popular support. Magnet schools and schools of choice provide rich opportunities for challenging the behavioral and programmatic regularities that have contributed to the dissociation of children from others and their own experience of the world. There is no guarantee that these new alternative programs will evolve in ways consistent with the arguments presented here, but they provide a space in which such experimentation could take place.

If economic and environmental conditions worsen over the next decades, it does not seem inconceivable that educators sensitive to these changes could convince parents of the value of a process of schooling that orients children to a recognition of their interdependence with others and the natural world. As indicated earlier, the phenomenon of capital flight (see Chapter 1) is creating situations not unlike those we might expect to encounter with a reduction in the forces of production. Throughout the United States, many previously functional communities have been abandoned by corporations that had provided the source of most economic support. If they wish to remain in their home communities, residents must turn to one another to develop new forms of economic development, dependent not upon the resources of multinational corporations but upon their own efforts. Schools could assume a pivotal role in helping economically displaced families achieve this end. In Pittsburgh, for example, educational experiments aimed at encouraging students and interested local adults to develop businesses within their own neighborhoods are currently being designed (Pittsburgh New Futures Proposal, 1988). The explicit goal of such experiments is community economic redevelopment. If such experiments prove successful, they could lead to greater parental commitment to education as well. Well-functioning training programs tied to schools might also serve to attract capital investment in more decentralized forms of economic activity.

Similarly, as the environmental crisis worsens, we may expect to see more citizens become willing to consider major changes in social relations and strategies for achieving personal security as they realize that such a transformation may be essential for their own well-being and that of their descendants. The efflorescence of the Green Movement in Western Europe appears to be tied to a growing recognition that the damage done to the natural world by our civilization will eventually come home to us (Galtung, 1986). Already, environmental organizations in the United States possess vast public support, at least in terms of membership and contributions (Borelli, 1988). This has not yet led to major shifts in lifestyles or patterns of consumption for large numbers of people. But as environmental conditions force us to adjust to new necessities—such as recycling, the use of sunscreens, regular examinations for skin cancer, the filtering of water, the avoidance of polluted beaches—recognizing the interrelationship between our own behaviors and the broader ecological systems in which we live will become inescapable. This situation could then result in a willingness on the part of more people to adopt environmentally viable social and economic practices.

The fact that some of the most effective efforts to halt environmental degradation are the result of citizen resistance to contemporary industrial or waste disposal practices that threaten the health of their communities demonstrates that when common people recognize a danger for what it is, they will respond (Commoner, 1987). Building upon that recognition, educators could develop schools that enable children to understand their place in broader systems and help them to acquire the economic, social, and political skills required to protect themselves from the activities of those who are insensitive to the damage they perpetrate on us, future generations, and the planet. In communities that have exhibited their willingness to act on these issues, parents might well be eager to sponsor the development of curricular and pedagogical reforms whose goal would be the cultivation of citizens capable of acting in ways that would guard the well-being of entire communities rather than just themselves.

Finally, although Americans have traditionally supported individual opportunity, freedom, and the uninhibited competitiveness that has become endemic in our social lives, they have also been believers in the importance of communal ties and justice. As the pendulum has swung to increasingly blatant demonstrations of selfishness and greed, public opinion has begun to turn away from excessive forms of possessive individualism. The highly materialistic lifestyle of many young professionals is not viewed as an undiluted good, but rather something that is both desired and derided. This ambivalence toward the pursuit of self-interest could possibly be built upon in an attempt to reassert other important American values such as the concern for others taught by Christianity and the civic responsibility central to Jeffersonian republicanism (Bellah, Madsen, Sullivan, Swidler, and Tipton, 1985).

A moral orientation directed at underlining the importance of fundamental ties to others thus already exists within our culture. An element of our common heritage not completely erased by the modern/industrial worldview, it remains a motif that could once again be raised to prominence. One task of educators concerned about developing a more appropriate form of schooling for our changed conditions would be to tap into this cultural reserve and unabashedly assert its importance as a means for helping us learn how to help one another through what may be a difficult period of adjustment.

Gaining the support of the general public for an educational model more directed to the welfare of the community and the natural environment, however, will undoubtedly encounter opposition from those who will continue to benefit from the forms of individualism and competition that characterize our current system. For the middle class, the training offered by schools facilitates, and for a time is likely to continue to facilitate, the placement of their children in professional and technical occupations largely at public expense. They can be expected to resist changes that threaten their ability to reproduce the advantages that accompany their class position. Efforts on the part of some educational spokespeople, especially powerful figures in the Department of Education during the Reagan years (Finn, 1987), have been directed toward the introduction of increased standardization and higher performance norms—reforms that will benefit children who, largely as a result of cultural advantages gained from their class backgrounds, often do well in school. Since it is members of the middle class who generally influence the nature of local educational practice, steps will need to be taken to convince them of the value of the changes outlined here. Doing so, especially as long as the benefits of educational training remain available to a sizable minority, may prove to be extraordinarily difficult.

As opportunities for those who possess advanced educational degrees diminish, however, fewer and fewer children from the middle class may in fact be able to benefit from their training. Already, competition to gain access to the most prestigious universities and colleges is fierce, and there is a growing belief on the part of middle-class parents that the next generation will not be able to enjoy their own material advantages. If this situation persists and the number of children from the middle class who are uable to realize their own occupational hopes becomes significantly reduced, it is possible that even members of the class most favored by public education will become willing to consider changes aimed at minimizing the forms of competition and detachment encountered in most classrooms.

As suggested earlier, children from lower- or working-class homes already face limited occupational possibilities. In the mid-1980s, a report from the Government Accounting Office revealed that the unemployment rate for black high school dropouts aged 16–24 was 70 percent. The unemployment rate for black high school graduates in the same age group was 67 percent (Government Accounting Office, 1986, 20). These figures point to the reality behind the statement made by a black middle-school student to the deputy mayor of Portland, Oregon, after being urged to graduate from high school: "Why bother? Look what it did for my brother. He's in jail. Look what it did for my dad. He's home watchin' TV. Why bother, man? I got a better chance makin' it on the streets, man" (Portland Investment, 1989, 1). Rectifying this situation can no longer be left to multinational corporations whose primary interest lies in reducing labor costs, rather than strengthening U.S. communities.

One of the few alternatives remaining to the poor is to create their own economic opportunities. This, of course, is what is now happening with the illegal drug trade. Ideally, economic practices such as those exhibited by the Mondragon cooperatives could also be used as a legitimate means for regenerating urban and rural areas depressed by the economic transformation that has occurred during the previous decade. An educational process that prepared children to participate in collective endeavors could conceivably play an instrumental role in fostering both the disposition and the will to consider such alternatives. If schools themselves became one locus for community regeneration, economically disadvantaged populations might come to support educational reforms such as the ones suggested here in the way they once supported efforts to desegregate public education.

As schools become increasingly unable to help children gain the social, practical, and academic skills needed to achieve security as adults, we can anticipate parental expectations regarding schooling to change. To some extent, this is already happening, though currently in ways that are generating higher rather than lower levels of competition. If members of the general public can be helped to see that the common good, as well as their own children, will be better served by schools which demonstrate the social support, engaging curriculum, and connection to the broader community now encountered in effective programs for at-risk youth, it may be possible to gain their support for the extension of such practices to more educational institutions. By building coalitions of parents that cross class lines, it may furthermore be possible to forge alliances with enough power and vision to pressure educators to change the schools.

Seeking the Support of Educators

Given their stake in the system of public schooling as it currently exists, educators are likely to be the most difficult group to convince that changes in school structures, pedagogical practice, and curriculum are necessary. As it has evolved throughout the twentieth century, the educational infrastructure militates against the formation of smaller, more humane, and organizationally autonomous schools—the kind of institutions that are more likely to foster the cooperation and mutual support discussed here. Before being changed, the old organizational model will have to be seen by educators as fundamentally inefficient and dysfunctional. Achieving this end is likely to result initially in denial, defensiveness, resistance, or resigned acceptance. The failure of a growing number of public schools to accomplish the tasks for which they were ostensibly designed, however, is becoming increasingly unacceptable not only to corporate leaders and the general public, but to some educators as well. As the dropout rates in major U.S. cities have risen to 50 and even up to 80 percent, teachers and school administrators have been hard-pressed to justify their current practice. If urban schools do not collapse altogether, it could be through attempts to meet the needs of students generally passed over in traditional classrooms that educators will implement more broadly the models of teaching and learning described in Chapter 6.

The Jefferson County School District in Louisville, Kentucky may exemplify the way in which such a transformation could occur in other places. In 1975, Louisville schools were forced to consolidate with schools throughout surrounding Jefferson County to comply with a desegregation order. The result was organizational chaos and a loss of faith in the ability of local schools to educate children. When a new superintendent took over the system in the early 1980s, he realized that regaining the support of corporate leaders and the general public would require demonstrating the schools' willingness to entertain profound changes to ensure the education of children who in the past had been allowed to fail. After a period of backing away from the schools, people in business realized that continued student failure would in the end affect their own productivity. They, too, then became willing to consider alternatives that had previously been marginal to conventional educational practice. Crisis thus inspired change.

In response to this situation, the district decided that to improve its schools it had to improve the quality of its teaching staff. It chose to do this through the creation of a professional development academy. The first step in this process involved locating people within the district who were already experimenting with innovative practices likely to increase student achievement and retention. During this year, schools were invited to participate in an effort to "invent" schools appropriate for the 21st century. If more than half of the educators in a given school expressed willingness to participate in this process, they could send three representatives to meet with colleagues from around the district who gathered regularly to consider an agenda to be carried out by what came to be called "professional development schools."

Twenty-four of the 150 schools in the Jefferson County School District agreed to participate in this process. During the spring of 1987, their representatives joined teachers appointed by the teachers' union, professors from the University of Louisville School of Education, central office administrators, and staff from the newly created Gheens Professional Development Academy to agree upon a set of foundational beliefs, orienting propositions, and standards against which participating schools would be evaluated. Before entering into this process, however, the group studied and discussed a number of materials related to school organization and culture. Central to the concept of professional development as it is being implemented in Louisville is a belief that educators must begin to reflect upon taken-for-granted practices and assumptions encountered in schools. Once they have begun to examine school culture as something that has been created rather than something which is inevitable, they are in a better position to reform their schools, freed at least partially from the self-censorship and narrow view of possible alternatives that often inhibit educational change (Sarason, 1982).

The foundational beliefs that arose from these discussions include the following:

I. Student success is the goal of all school activity.
II. Students need to be challenged and need to learn to pursue difficult tasks and persist with tasks at which they are unsuccessful.
III. Learning is an active process.
IV. Teachers are leaders, and principals are leaders of leaders.
V. The business of the school district and the state is to assure that each school unit operates under optimal conditions and produces optimal results.
VI. Staff success results from motivated and competent people working in an environment that is committed to their success, continuing growth, and development (Schlechty, Ingwerson, and Brooks, 1988, 30).

Although the vision of the Louisville reform movement superficially has little to do with the vision of interdependence that has informed this book, the commitment to the success of all students in the district has engendered reforms very much in keeping with those discussed earlier.

Closely involved in the initial start-up of this reform process was an educator named Terry Brooks. Brooks had been the principal at Noe Middle School when Lipsitz (1984) chose it as an exemplary model of middle-school restructuring. In the late 1970s, Noe began experimenting with organizational clustering, expanded roles for teachers, an administrative process that focused on staff support rather than supervision, and curricular and pedagogical reforms aimed at eliciting higher levels of educational engagement among its primarily poor and working-class students. In 1974, prior to the introduction of these reforms, students' scores ranged from the first through third stanines on the California Test of Basic Skills. By 1981, the average student score had risen to the fifth stanine; variance in performance had also narrowed (Lipsitz, 1984, 94). What Brooks and his fellow educators were able to demonstrate to their colleagues throughout the district was the effectiveness of their methods. By creating a caring and stimulating educational environment, they had been able to reverse patterns of failure so often encountered among at-risk youth.

Though the educational practices encountered at Noe Middle School may as yet remain an anomaly in most schools in Jefferson County (Timar, 1989), the activities of innovative educators at the

Gheens Academy promise to introduce more of their colleagues to alternative practices they have implemented and experienced. If more teachers encounter the success these innovators have known in enhancing student performance, it seems likely that such reforms might become rooted in other schools as well. In the first six years of this reform movement, 15 elementary schools, 14 middle schools, and 11 high schools initiated serious efforts to restructure their programs (Kyle, 1988, 11).

As a reform process, the Jefferson County experience offers important lessons to educators concerned about fostering a fundamental transformation of the schools. Although it is too early to judge whether this effort will ultimately result in the restructuring sought by the staff at the Gheens Academy, the activity that has been generated in and around Louisville since 1983 is encouraging. As educators focus on supporting the successful learning of all students, it seems likely that they will turn to school structures, pedagogical practices, and curricula that connect children to the act of teaching and learning. The structures, practices, and curricula they choose could then contribute to the experience of interdependence presented as so important here. In this manner, current concerns about the schooling of educationally disadvantaged students may lead teachers and principals to implement reforms that could help to reshape schools in ways that will be more appropriate for the changed material conditions that now seem to await us.

Conclusion

It may be a number of years before the perspective regarding the future of modern/industrial civilization presented here is shared by more than a handful of people. The weight of our lived experience in a culture that seems so solid and inevitable makes projections of its devolution appear implausible. Still, growing unease among populations in industrialized nations about the environmental consequences of our actions, and the precariousness of economic growth predicated on debt rather than productivity indicate that widespread faith in our way of life and the ineluctability of progress is no longer as secure as it once was. If such sentiments become translated into broad-based citizen action, then the value of an educational process that furthers the experience and recognition of interdependence and mutual support may become more apparent.

The development of such an educational agenda, however, may depend upon its being linked to a more comprehensive economic and political agenda focused on the issues raised in Chapter 4. To be successful, schools aimed at developing concern about the social collective and the broader environment must be part of a larger social vision. In other words, there must be communities of people who share a vision of the world that schools should prepare children to inhabit, communities that furthermore are willing to take a hand in shaping that world. This kind of broad economic and political movement does not yet exist in the United States, and it will be difficult if not impossible to implement an educational program based on the premises outlined here until such a movement has gained a significant following.

The question then arises, what can be done now? Because of the importance of the formation of a broad-based social movement, educators must direct part of their attention and energy to the efforts of those who are working for the development of environmental policies more sensitive to the planet's limits, economic and political decentralization, and the rights of peoples on the margins of Western civilization. These cultures may have much to teach us about survival in a world where energy will no longer be cheap and the conveniences of our own way of life no longer as easily available. At present, activities in regard to these issues are fragmented. They need to be brought together into a unified whole if they are to assume any political significance in the United States. The Green Movement in Europe has achieved a major share of its success because of the way in which people concerned about a variety of different political problems have been able to establish consolidated action groups. Though the European Green Movement remains troubled by infighting and dissension, its continued growth over the past decade is cause for guarded hope. In the United States, those of us concerned about the issues raised here should attempt to transform those concerns into an increasingly inclusive social movement aimed at the articulation and creation of an alternative society, one capable of fostering both sustainability and economic justice.

In regard to schools as they currently exist, the strategy outlined in this and the previous chapter may present one vehicle for encouraging the development of an educational process more likely to nurture cooperation and collective responsibility. Although the creation of programs for educationally disadvantaged students ultimately remains tied to the transmission of values, attributes, and abilities desired by an economy predicated on growth rather than sustainability, inherent contradictions in the structure of capitalism are forcing us to recognize that the forms of economic and political centralization that have contributed to the growth and wealth of our civilization may have reached a point of diminishing returns. The decentralization of production and of the delivery of governmental services is now being regarded in a much more favorable light than previously. Schools are already beginning to experience the implications of these altered perspectives in calls for the creation of smaller programs, more individualized attention, site-based governance, and the streamlining of school administration. Although much of the school reform literature over the past decade remains highly contradictory, strands of thought encountered there could form the warp upon which education for interdependence could eventually be woven.

Our task today is to affirm and extend measures we believe would contribute to the development of schools that demonstrate to children their attachment to one another and the world in which they live. Our rhetoric may well need to be focused not on issues related to the environment or an increasingly inequitable economy, but upon the need to ensure the success of all students. Although predicated on persistent assumptions about the importance of individual economic mobility, the desire to ensure that success is indicative of a recognition that self-interest is intimately linked to the interest of others. In the past, the failure or minimal attainment of a majority of students in fact served the interests of those who benefited most from our economic and social structures. Now, however, the well-being of the privileged rests on the success of the disadvantaged. Changes in the nature of the world economy are making explicit the interdependence of socioeconomic classes, an interdependence that has always existed but could be easily denied in circumstances more favorable to American owners and managers. What appears to be a threat to the viability of the U.S. economy in a global market could be turned into an opportunity to initiate educational reforms capable of nurturing an ethic grounded in concern for the common good rather than individual mobility. Although it may be premature to link educational reforms to the cultivation of such an ethic, the development of social skills that foster cooperation, group problem solving, initiative, and commitment to others will be viewed with favor. For a time, these skills could serve the continued expansion and health of an economy whose days may be limited. Such skills, however, will also have great value if and when they need to be turned to the work of creating a more sustainable culture.

I do not wish to imply that any of this will be easy, nor that the efforts of educators will even be of much significance in the process of making a transition to a world that may be very different from the one we know now. The work that lies ahead appears truly over-whelming. It will need to be accomplished in the midst of social and ecological crises that could be disruptive on a scale far more devastating than anything human beings have had to grapple with in the past. In part, this will be so because of the global nature of current problems, the fragility of a lifestyle dependent upon scarce resources, and the vast numbers of people who now inhabit the planet. My hope, however, is that children prepared to deal with these problems collectively rather than individually will be in a better position to seek solutions cognizant of the needs and desires of others. By recognizing their shared interests, they may be more likely to approach their situation not as defensive and frightened social atoms, but as associations of people capable of pooling their combined talents and energies to create responses to new physical and social conditions—responses that will be both compassionate and just. I have no illusions about the possibility that large numbers of people will almost certainly react with fear and violence to the events that may await us. Such a response seems far more likely than the agenda I have presented here. Still, it is in this or another less plausible agenda that the well-being of our species may lie. Children who have experienced the possibilities of cooperation may be more likely to cooperate.

In the past, human communities able to persist in the same region over time did so because of their insistence that the next generation master patterns of interaction that respected and sustained surrounding social and natural environments. The luxury of modernization has made such patterns appear vestigial. As we prepare to return to conditions that may once again demand cooperation and the subordination of self-interest to the needs of the collective, it will be important to convey to the young social relations that affirm connectedness and mutual responsibility. If these lessons are not instilled, we may truly find ourselves in the Hobbesian nightmare of each against all. To the teaching of those lessons we must direct our energies and our lives.

Notes

Chapter One

1. Writing in the 1970s, Heilbroner argued that socialist countries would face a similar crisis. Socialism, like capitalism, is dependent on a continued expansion of the forces of production. Heilbroner believed that because of their collectivist nature, socialist societies would be able to make a smoother transition to the more sustainable and frugal economic order that awaits us. As it has turned out, political developments in the late 1980s and early 1990s have demonstrated that declines in productivity coupled to public outrage regarding environmental destruction (e.g., protests about the disasters at Chernobyl and the Aral Sea) can contribute to the disintegration of state apparatuses previously thought to be stable and virtually implacable. Rather than outlasting their capitalist counterparts, Eastern bloc countries are experiencing events that may foreshadow developments in the West.

Chapter Two

1. It must be noted that different cultures have responded to the industrial and scientific revolutions in various ways. Japan and Korea, for example, have accepted Western industrial practices without as yet diminishing the importance of smaller human associations such as the family and workgroup (Mollner, 1988). In these countries, productivity does not depend upon the forms of entrepreneurial capitalism that sparked and sustained the industrial revolution through the mid-twentieth century. Rather, productivity is linked to feudalistic social patterns that stress loyalty, obligation, and a sensitivity to the needs of others, patterns that seem particularly well-suited to the phase of corporate capitalism we have now entered.

The individualism that has become such a dominant feature in Western industrial countries is as yet not much in evidence in these Asian nations. Workers are motivated to produce not so much for themselves as for their families and their companies. Their identities are closely linked to the identities of those around them. In this important sense, the modern/industrial worldview described in this chapter is not applicable to Japan and Korea. Ketcham (1987) deals with this issue at length in his study of the impact of individualism on public life in the United States.

Despite the greater emphasis placed upon the well-being of the community as opposed to the well-being of the self in industrialized Asian nations, however, it is hard to predict what the long-term impact of rationalism and empiricism, the breakdown of traditional social customs and roles, and the ideology of progress may have on citizens of these countries. The liberation of women from their traditional roles as primary caregivers of children, for example, could potentially have a powerful impact upon the degree of embeddedness new generations of Japanese and Korean people experience in regard to their families and communities. Johnson (1973) and Leestma (1987), for example, point to the pivotal role played by Japanese mothers in socializing their children to subordinate their own needs to the needs of others. If Japanese mothers no longer have the time or the inclination to play this role, it does not seem unlikely that the individualism that has become problematic in the West could also become so in the East.

2. Marshall Sahlins (1972) in *Stone Age Economics*, however, has argued that a higher proportion of the earth's population was adequately housed and fed during the Paleolithic period than in our own. People during this era apparently possessed much more time to engage in social and artistic pursuits as well.

3. It goes without saying that millions of Americans have not been able to achieve such security, but the possibility of doing so has been a fundamental component of our national ideology. It is this ideology and the social institutions that have grown up around it that are being challenged by the ecological crises of the late twentieth century.

Chapter Three

1. It is important to note that the family and neighborhood environments in which children experience affection and mutual support are no longer as common as they once were. Without that experience, children often do not possess what Dreeben describes as "the necessary social and psychological support from sources outside the school or sufficient inner resources to cope with the demands of schooling" (1968, 84). Ironically, elements of the modern/industrial world that encourage social detachment and individualism are now contributing to the breakdown of institutions within which individuals were once able to construct a sense of their own identity and purpose. This development provides an additional rationale for developing schools that replicate rather than replace the social relations encountered in well-functioning primary groups and communities.

2. This is not to say, however, that school officials do not attempt to create a broader sense of group identity. Waller (1932/1967) also notes, for example, that interscholastic athletic competition is specifically aimed at engendering this kind of student solidarity. Such solidarity, however, is defined in the school's terms, not the students'. In a subtle way, these controlled organizations serve to divert student attention away from the formation of more spontaneous associations capable of developing a degree of independence from the school and then challenging its agenda and authority.

Chapter Four

1. Francis Crick, the codiscoverer of DNA, has said: "The ultimate aim of the modern movement in biology is to explain all biology in terms of physics and chemistry" (in Smith, 1982, 136).

2. In making reference to the patterns of familial and communal social organization that existed prior to the modern era, both here and in subsequent passages, I do not mean to imply that these patterns were not problematic. They frequently demonstrate forms of patriarchy and class discrimination that have been the legitimate objects of modern reform efforts. The construction of smaller human associations in the future does not need to replicate these earlier patterns of injustice. This is not to suggest that avoiding them will be simple. I only mean to say that it is not beyond the realm of possibility.

3. Banfield (1958) and Fromm and Maccoby (1975) describe peasant societies in which individualism is as pronounced as in our own. The phenomenon occurs when economic conditions are such that cooperative activities are unable to result in positive outcomes that increase physical security and well-being.

4. Erikson (1976) also describes the fragility of these mechanisms. After experiencing a devastating flood, residents of the Buffalo Creek drainage were unable to reestablish the patterns of support that had previously sustained them. Without that communal support, many became painfully insecure and depressed. Erikson further posits that access to governmental aid inhibited the restoration of former patterns of mutual aid among resettled neighbors, thus offering some credence to the rationale behind Amish resistance to Social Security.

Chapter Five

1. Heath (1983) and Wigginton (1985) describe learning activities that require students to become researchers in their own neighborhoods. Newmann and Rutter (1985a, 1985b) provide a useful overview of different community service programs that are now in operation in a number of schools around the United States, as well as an analysis of their impact on students. Foley and McConnaughy (1982) describe the use of internships at the City-as-School in New York City. In their description of the Jefferson County Open High School in Evergreen, Colorado, Gregory and Smith (1987) and Horwood (1987) demonstrate how one school has successfully integrated all these activities into its program following the Walkabout model developed by Maurice Gibbons (1974, 1984).

2. Bronfenbrenner (1970) discusses the importance of integrating nonschool adults in educational programs and describes a number of ways this

was accomplished in Soviet schools. Turkel and Abramson (1986) offer one model for how comparable mentoring programs can be introduced into American schools.

3. Educators in Native American schools have been particularly active in attempting to develop programs that honor their students' culture and yet acquaint them with elements of the dominant culture necessary for their participation in the mainstream economy. Rutter (1987) describes the program of the NA-WAY-EE school in Minneapolis, where social studies, language, science, and art classes approach their disciplines through a Native American cultural lens. Parent (1985) reviews a text written by people of the Rock Point Community School on the Navajo reservation. This text, *Between Sacred Mountains: Navajo Stories and Lessons from the Land* (1984) functions as a curriculum in history, science, and social studies. It describes the relationship of the Navajo people to their land, utilizing instructional forms such as storytelling to convey this Indian nation's history and lore. Jordan (1985) discusses the way adapting instructional practices to match the social relations encountered in the homes of native Hawaiian children resulted in more successful learning outcomes at the Kamehameha School in Honolulu.

4. Raizen (1988) has written about the value of inquiry-based curricula, stressing that children master the principles that lie behind scientific disciplines not through memorizing definitions, facts, and theories, but through their own investigatory activities. Cohen (1986) has shown how these investigations are even more meaningful for students when they are carried out in small groups. Sizer (1986) has similarly argued that students must be seen as "knowledge workers" rather than knowledge recipients whose learning is directed at the exploration of questions deemed to be "essential" by their teachers.

5. Madden et al. (1989) describe the successful use of reading tutors in an inner-city Baltimore elementary school as a means for providing additional adult support for children having difficulty mastering basic academic skills. Farber (1988) discusses the advisory program at Central Park East Secondary School. In this program, students spend four hours a week in an advisory period. All school adults, including the principal, are assigned to such a group, which normally consists of 12 to 15 students. The main point of the period is to "give each student and family a person in the school who knows the child fully. Each teacher has an advisory period and these students become his special charge" (6).

6. Ratzki (1988) describes the structure of some West German schools in which students remain with the same team of five to eight teachers for up to six years, an approach that facilitates long-term support, care, and accountability.

7. Gregory and Smith (1987) and Horwood (1987) show how students have been brought successfully into the process of school governance at the

Jefferson County Open High School. Purpel (1989) describes a similar process at the Brookline High School in Boston, where a town meeting composed of 50 people (44 students, four teachers, and two cafeteria workers) deal with issues such as attendance policies, curriculum requirements, staff hiring, discipline, and exam schedules (161). Hand (1989) discusses the implementation of Kohlberg's "just community" model at the Theodore Roosevelt High School in the Bronx. In each instance students have been given a significant role in decisions that affect the life of the entire school.

8. In the West German schools discussed by Ratzki (1988), students remain with the same group of approximately 80–90 students as well as the same team of teachers from the fourth through tenth grades. Some middle schools in the United States are currently experimenting with similar structures, although not of the same duration (Lipsitz 1984).

9. Ratzki (1988) also describes the utilization of cooperative learning groups in the West German schools with which she is associated. Students remain in the same groups of five to six children for a year or more. They work with one another in all subject areas. Ratzki notes that more academically able students often take an active role in assisting peers who have trouble mastering material by consulting outside their group with other strong students about effective teaching strategies. Bronfenbrenner (1970) similarly describes the importance of peer instruction in Soviet schools. Peer tutoring is another effective strategy for eliciting student-student interaction and mutual support. Cohen, Kulik, and Kulik (1982) provide a meta-analysis of findings about this instructional strategy.

10. Deutsch's (1962) complete definition follows:

In a competitive situation, the goals for the individuals are *contriently interdependent*. "Contrient interdependence" is the condition in which individuals are so linked together that there is a negative correlation between their goal attainments.... In the limiting case, under complete contrient interdependence an individual can attain his goal if and only if the others with whom he is linked cannot attain their goals. A psychological state of competition implies the perception of contrient interdependence; the interpersonal state of competition implies mutual perception of this state. (276)

11. It must be acknowledged that the educational practices encountered in many socialist countries are aimed at diminishing ties to primary groups in an attempt to align children with the State or nation (Makarenko, 1976). From my own perspective, such an agenda may be misguided in that it can direct children's attention away from more immediate social responsibilities and obligations. Coupled with this attempted redirection of affiliation away from local groups has been a centralization of power and decision making at the national level that has tended to lead to the political and economic alienation of average citizens within some socialist countries (Eshete, 1981). Despite

these drawbacks, practices described by Bronfenbrenner (1970) and Cagan (1978) still seem appropriate for the development of an educational model more likely to lead to cooperative rather than competitive social relations.

Chapter Six

1. Descriptions of the following three schools are drawn from unpublished case studies written during the course of research at the National Center on Effective Secondary Schools, University of Wisconsin-Madison. They are collected in a volume entitled *Dropout Prevention and Recovery: Fourteen Case Studies* (1987). This research was conducted by a team of five people at 15 different schools for at-risk youth (one withdrew before the completion of the study) during the 1986–87 school year. Three visits of approximately five working days each were scheduled to most sites. Research at the Madison School-Within-a-School and Sierra Mountain High School was conducted by the author. The research methodology for this study included participant observation of classes, staff meetings, student conferences, extracurricular activities, and internship programs; extensive interviewing of students, teachers, administrators, counselors, and others associated with the programs; review of student records; and the administration of instruments to measure academic achievement (the Degrees of Reading Power and writing samples) and social attitudes (the Wisconsin Youth Survey). These case studies formed the basis of the book summarizing this research project, *Reducing the Risk: Schools as Communities of Support* (Wehlage et al., 1989).

2. After the establishment of a publicly supported high school in the area in the 1980s, St. Mary's was closed. Regardless of this fact, previous practices at this school remain useful as a model of an educational process more likely to engender in students an experience of interdependence and social responsibility.

Chapter Seven

1. As reported in Hanh (1987) and Hanh et al. (1987), educators have identified the following components of successful programs for at-risk children:

[M]entorships and intensive, sustained counseling for troubled youngsters;

an array of social services, including health care, family planning education, and infant care facilities for adolescent mothers;

concentrated remediation using individualized instruction and competency-based curricula;

an effective school/business collaboration that provides ongoing access to the mainstream economy;

improved incentives, including financial rewards, for completing high school;

year-round schools and alternative schools;

heightened accountability for dropout rates at all levels of the system of public education;

involvement of parents and community organizations in dropout prevention. (260-61).

Although not all these components incorporate the emphasis on social relations and active engagement in learning that have been my focus here, nearly all are aimed at enhancing student-adult relationships and linking schools more clearly to the broader community and students' out-of-school lives.

Bibliography

Anyon, Jean. 1981. Social class and school knowledge. *Curriculum Inquiry* 11, no.1:3–42.

Apple, Michael W. 1979. *Ideology and curriculum.* London: Routledge and Kegan Paul.

Apple, Michael W. 1982. *Education and power.* Boston: Ark.

Bahro, Rudolf. 1986. *Building the Green movement.* Philadelphia: New Society Publishers.

Banfield, Edward C. 1958. *The moral basis of a backward society.* New York: Free Press.

Barker, Roger G., and Gump, Paul V. 1964. *Big school, small school: High school size and student behavior.* Stanford, CA: Stanford University Press.

Bellah, Robert N; Madsen, Richard; Sullivan, William M; Swidler, Ann; Tipton, Steven M. 1985. *Habits of the heart: Individualism and commitment in American life.* New York: Harper and Row.

Bender, Thomas. 1978. *Community and social change in America.* Baltimore: Johns Hopkins University Press.

Berman, Marshall. 1982/1988. *All that is solid melts into air: The experience of modernity.* New York: Penguin.

Berman, Morris. 1981. *The reenchantment of the world.* Ithaca: Cornell University Press.

Bernstein, Basil. 1975. *Class, codes, and control: Volume 3, towards a theory of educational transmissions.* London: Routledge and Kegan Paul.

Blank, Rolf K. 1987. Comparative analysis of local planning and development of magnet schools. Washington, D.C.: Office of Educational Research and Improvement.

————. 1989. *Educational effects of magnet high schools.* Madison, WI; National Center on Effective Secondary Schools.

Boggs, Carl. 1986. *Social movements and political power: Emerging forms of radicalism in the West.* Philadelphia: Temple University Press.

Bookchin, Murray. 1980. *Toward an ecological society*. Montreal, Canada: Black Rose Books.

Borelli, Peter. 1988. The ecophilosophers. *Amicus Journal* (Spring):30–39.

Borman, Kathryn M.; Mueninghoff, Elaine; and Piazza, Shirley. 1988. Urban Appalachian girls and young women: Bowing to no one. In Lois Weis (Ed.), *Cultural Forms in School*. Albany: State University of New York Press.

Bowers, C. A. 1987. *Elements of a post-liberal theory of education*. New York: Teachers College Press.

Bowles, Samuel, and Gintis, Herbert. 1976. *Schooling in capitalist America: Educational reform and the contradictions of economic life*. New York: Basic Books.

————. 1986. *Democracy and capitalism: Property, community, and the contradiction of modern social thought*. New York: Basic Books.

Brandt, Ron. 1987. On cooperation in schools: A conversation with David and Roger Johnson. *Educational Leadership* (November):14–18.

Bronfenbrenner, Urie. 1970. *Two worlds of childhood*. New York: Simon and Schuster.

————. 1986. Alienation and the four worlds of childhood. *Phi Delta Kappan* 67 (February):430–36.

Brown, Lester R., and Postel, Sandra. 1987. Thresholds of change. In Lester R. Brown (Ed.), *State of the world: 1987*, 3–19. New York and London: Norton.

Buber, Martin. 1958. *I and thou*. New York: Scribner.

Cagan, Elizabeth. 1978. Individualism, collectivism, and radical educational reform. *Harvard Educational Review* 48:2 (May):227–66.

Capra, Fritjof. 1983. *The turning point: Science, society, and the rising culture*. New York: Bantam Books.

Capra, Fritjof, and Spretnak, Charlene. 1984. *Green politics*. New York: E. P. Dutton.

Carnoy, Martin, and Levin, Henry M. 1985. *Schooling and work in the democratic state*. Stanford, CA: Stanford University Press.

Catterall, James S. 1987. On the social costs of dropping out of school. *The High School Journal* (October/November):19–30.

Chance, Norman A. 1966. *The Eskimo of north Alaska*. New York: Holt, Rinehart, and Winston.

Church, Robert L., and Sedlak, Michael W. 1976. *Education in the United States: An interpretive history*. New York: Free Press.

Clark, Mary E. 1989. *Ariadne's thread: The search for new modes of thinking*. London: Macmillan.

Coates, Gary J. 1981. *Resettling America: Energy, ecology, and community*. Andover, MA: Brick House Publishing Company.

Cohen, Elizabeth. 1986. *Designing groupwork: Strategies for the heterogeneous classroom*. New York: Teachers College Press.

Cohen, G. A. 1978. *Karl Marx's theory of history: A defense*. Princeton, NJ: Princeton University Press.

Cohen, Peter; Kulick, James A.; and Kulick, Chen-Lin. 1982. Educational outcomes of tutoring: A meta-analysis of findings. *American Educational Research Journal* 19, no. 2 (Summer):237–48.

Coleman, James S., and Hoffer, Thomas. 1987. *Public and private high schools: The impact of communities*. New York: Basic Books.

College Board. 1983. *Academic preparation for college: What students need to know and be able to do*. New York: College Entrance Examinations.

Collier, John. 1973. *Alaskan Eskimo education*. New York: Holt, Rinehart, and Winston.

Collins, Randall. 1979. *The credential society: An historical sociology of education and stratification*. New York: Academic Press.

Combs, Arthur W. 1988. New assumptions for educational reform. *Educational Leadership* 45 (February):38–40.

Comer, James P. 1988. Educating poor minority children. *Scientific American* 259, no. 5:42–48.

Committee for Economic Development. 1987. *Children in need: Investment strategies for the educationally disadvantaged*. New York.

Commoner, Barry. 1987. The environment. *New Yorker* 63 (June 16, 1987):46–47+.

Connell, R. W.; Ashenden, D. J.; Kessler, S.; and Dowsett, G. W. 1982. *Making the difference: Schools, families, and social division*. Sydney: George Allen and Unwin.

Council of Chief State School Officers. 1987. *Elements of a model state statute to provide educational entitlements for at-risk students*. Washington, D.C.: Author.

———. 1989. *Success for all in a new century*. Washington, D.C.: The Council.

Cusick, Philip. 1973. *Inside high school: The students' world*. New York: Holt, Rinehart, and Winston.

Dale, Roger. 1982. Education and the capitalist state: Contributions and contradictions. In Michael W. Apple (Ed.), *Cultural and economic reproduction in
education*, 127–61. Boston: Routledge and Kegan Paul.

Dallmayr, Fred R. 1981. *Twilight of subjectivity: Contributions to a post-individual-
ist theory of politics*. Amherst: University of Massachusetts Press.

Daly, Herman F., and Cobb, John B. 1989. *For the common good: Redirecting the
economy toward community, the environment, and a sustainable future*. Boston:
Beacon.

David, Jane L.; Purkey, Stewart S.; and White, Paula. 1989. *Restructuring in
progress: Lessons from pioneering districts*. Washington, D.C.: National Governors' Association, Center for Policy Research.

Davies, Lynn. 1984. *Pupil power: Deviance and gender in school*. Lewes, Great
Britain: Falmer Press.

deLone, Richard H. 1987. *State governments and at-risk youth: The critical link*.
Philadelphia: Public/Private Ventures.

D'Souza, Corinne K. 1989. A new movement, a new hope: East wind, west
wind, and the wind from the south. In Judith Plant (Ed.), *Healing the
wounds: The promise of ecofeminism*, 29–39. Philadelphia: New Society Publishers.

Deutsch, Martin. 1962. Cooperation and trust: Some theoretical notes. In M. R.
Jones (Ed.), *Nebraska symposium on motivation*, 275–319. Lincoln: University of Nebraska Press.

Devall, Bill. 1980. The deep ecology movement. *Natural Resources Journal*
20:299–322.

Devall, Bill, and Sessions, George. 1985. *Deep Ecology*. Layton, Utah: Gibbs M.
Smith.

Dewey, John. 1916/1966. *Democracy and education*. New York: Free Press.

———. 1927. *The public and its problems*. New York: Holt and Company.

———. 1929. *Individualism old and new*. New York: Capricorn Books.

———. 1959. *Dewey on education*. Martin S. Dworkin (Ed.). New York: Teachers
College Press.

Dreeben, Robert. 1968. *On what is learned in school*. Reading, MA: Addison-
Wesley.

———. 1977. The contribution of schooling to learning of norms. In Jerome
Karabel and A. H. Halsey (Eds.), *Power and ideology in education*. New
York: Oxford University Press.

Dreyfus, Hubert L., and Rabineau, Paul. 1982. *Michel Foucault: Beyond structuralism and hermeneutics*. Chicago: University of Chicago Press.

Duckworth, Eleanor. 1991. Twenty-four, forty-two, and I love you: Keeping it complex. *Harvard Educational Review* 61, no. 1 (February):1–24.

Durkheim, Emile. 1925/1961. *Moral education: A study in the theory and application of the sociology of education*. Translated by Everett K. Wilson and Herman Schnurer. New York: Free Press.

Durning, Alan. 1991. Asking how much is enough. In Lester Brown (Ed.), *State of the world: 1991*. New York and London: Norton.

Eisenstadt, S. N. 1956. *From generation to generation*. New York: Free Press.

Elmore, Richard F. 1983. Social policymaking as strategic intervention. In E. Seidman (Ed.), *Social intervention*, 212–36. Beverly Hills, CA: Sage.

Erikson, Kai T. 1976. *Everything in its path: Destruction of community in the Buffalo Creek flood*. New York: Simon and Schuster.

Eshete, Andreas. 1981. Fraternity. *Review of Metaphysics* 35 (September):27–44.

Esland, Geoffrey M. 1971. Teaching and learning as the organization of knowledge. In Michael F.D. Young (Ed.), *Knowledge and control: New directions for the sociology of education*, 70–115. London: Collier-Macmillian.

Everhart, Robert B. 1983. *Reading, writing, and resistance: Adolescence and labor in a junior high school*. Boston: Routledge and Kegan Paul.

Farber, Peggy. 1988. Central Park East: High school with a human face. *Rethinking Schools* 2, no. 4 (May/June):6–7.

Fine, Michelle, and Zane, Nancie. 1989. Bein' wrapped too tight: When low-income women drop out of high school. In Lois Weis, Eleanor Farrar, and Hugh G. Petrie (Eds.), *Dropouts from school: Issues, dilemmas, and solutions*. Albany: State University of New York Press.

Finn, Chester E. 1987. The high school dropout puzzle. *Public Interest* (Spring):3–22.

Fiske, Edward B. 1989. The global imperative. *New York Times* (April 9, 1989), Section 4A:18–19.

Floud, Jean, and Halsey, A.H. 1959. Education and social structure: Theories and methods. *Harvard Educational Review* 29, no. 4 (Fall):288–96.

Foley, Eileen M. and McConnaughy, Susan B. 1982. *Towards school improvement: Lessons from alternative high schools*. New York: Public Education Association.

Fordham, Signithia. 1988. Racelessness as a factor in black students' school success: Pragmatic strategy or Pyrric victory? *Harvard Educational Review* 58, no. 1 (Feburary):54–84.

Fordham, Signithia, and Ogbu, John U. 1986. Black students' school success: Coping with the burden of "acting white." *The Urban Review* 18, no. 3:176–205.

Foucault, Michel. 1977. *Discipline and punish*. Translated by Alan Sheridan. New York: Vintage Books.

Fromm, Erich and Maccoby, Michael. 1976. A Mexican peasant village, in Donald W. Oliver, *Education and community: A radical critique of innovative schooling*. Berkeley: McCutchan.

Fullan, Michael. 1982. *The meaning of educational change*. New York: Teachers College Press.

Galtung, Johan. 1986. The Green movement: A socio-historical explanation. *International Sociology* 1, no. 1:75–90.

Gans, Herbert J. 1962. *The urban villagers: Group and class in the life of Italian-Americans*. New York: Free Press.

———. 1988. *Middle American individualism: The future of liberal democracy*. New York: Free Press.

Gardner, Howard. 1983. *Frames of mind: the theory of multiple intelligences*. New York: Basic Books.

Gearing, Fred O., and Epstein, Paul. 1982. Learning to wait: An ethnographic probe into the operations of an item of hidden curriculum. In George Spindler (Ed.), *Doing the ethnography of schooling*, 240–67. New York: Holt, Rinehart, and Winston.

Gibbons, Maurice. 1974. Walkabout: Searching for the right passage from childhood and school. *Phi Delta Kappan* 55 (May):596–602.

———. 1984. Walkabout ten years later: Searching for a renewed vision of education. *Phi Delta Kappan* 65, no. 9 (May):591–600.

Goldstein, Beth L. 1985. *School for cultural transitions: Hmong girls and boys in American high schools*. Unpublished dissertation, University of Wisconsin-Madison.

Goodlad, John I. 1984. *A place called school: Prospects for the future*. New York: McGraw-Hill.

Government Accounting Office. 1986. *School dropouts: The extent and nature of the problem*. Washington, D.C.: U.S. Government Printing Office.

Gracey, Harry L. 1972. *Curriculum or craftsmanship: Elementary school teachers in a bureaucratic system*. Chicago: University of Chicago Press.

Green Party of Federal Republic of Germany. 1985. *The program of the Green party of the Federal Republic of Germany*. Koln, West Germany: Farbo.

Green, Thomas F. 1980. *Predicting the behavior of the educational system*. Syracuse: Syracuse University Press.

Gregory, Thomas B., and Smith, Gerald R. 1987. *High schools as communities: The small school reconsidered*. Bloomington, IN: Phi Delta Kappa Educational Foundation.

Hamby, John V. 1989. How to get an "A" on your dropout prevention report card. *Educational Leadership* 46, no. 5 (February):21–23.

Hand, Douglas. 1989. Morality lessons? Hear! Hear! *New York Times* (April 9, 1989), Section 4A:53.

Hanh, Andrew. 1987. Reaching out to America's dropouts: What to do? *Phi Delta Kappan* (December):256–63.

Hanh, Andrew; Danzberger, Jacqueline; and Lefkowitz, Bernard. 1987. *Dropouts in America: Enough is known for action*. Institute for Educational Leadership.

Hardin, Garrett. 1968. The tragedy of the commons. *Science* 162 (December):1243–48.

Heath, Shirley Brice. 1983. *Ways with words: Language, life, and work in communities and classrooms*. New York: Cambridge University Press.

Heilbroner, Robert. 1980. *An inquiry into the human prospect*. New York: Norton.

Herberg, Will. 1961. Religion and education in America. In James Ward Smith and A. Leland Jamison (Eds.), *Religious perspectives in American schooling*. Princeton, NJ: Princeton University Press.

Herndon, James. 1965. *The way it spozed to be*. New York: Simon and Schuster.

Hobbes, Thomas. 1651/1962. *Leviathan; Or the matter, forme, and power of a commonwealth ecclesiasticall and civil*. New York: Collier.

Hodgkinson, Harold. 1988. The right kids for the right stuff. *Educational Leadership* (February):10–14.

Hodgkinson, Harold , and Mirga, Tom. 1986. Here they come, ready or not. *Education Week* 5, no. 34 (May 14):13–37.

Hogan, David. 1982. Education, economy, and the state. In Michael W. Apple (Ed.), *Cultural and economic reproduction in education: Essays on class, ideology and the state*. Boston: Routledge and Kegan Paul.

Horwood, Bert. 1987. *Experiential education in high school: Life in the walkabout program.* Boulder, CO: Association for Experiential Education.

Hostetler, John A. 1963. *Amish society.* Baltimore: Johns Hopkins Press.

Hostetler, John A., and Huntington, Gertrude Enders. 1971. *Children in Amish society: Socialization and community education.* New York: Holt, Rinehart, and Winston.

Ignatieff, Michael. 1984. *The needs of strangers: An essay on privacy, solidarity, and the politics of being human.* New York: Penguin.

Inkeles, Alex, and Smith, David. 1974. *Becoming modern: Individual change in six developing countries.* Cambridge: Harvard University Press.

Jackson, Philip W. 1968. *Life in classrooms.* New York: Holt, Rinehart, and Winston.

Johnson, Colleen Leahy. 1973. Alternatives to alienation: A Japanese-American example. In Frank Johnson (Ed.), *Alienation: Concept, term, and meanings.* New York: Seminar Press.

Johnson, David W., and Johnson, Roger T. 1974. Instructional goal structure: Cooperative, competitive, or individualistic. *Review of Educational Research* 44, no. 2:213–40.

Johnston, William B. 1987. *Workforce 2000: Work and workers for the 21st century.* Indianapolis: Hudson Institute.

Jordan, Cathie. 1985. Translating culture: From ethnographic information to educational program. *Anthropology and Education Quarterly* 16, no. 2 (Summer):105–23.

Kaestle, Carl. 1985. Education reform and the swinging pendulum. *Phi Delta Kappan* (February).

Katz, Michael B. 1971. *Class, bureaucracy, and schools: The illusion of educational change in America.* New York: Praeger.

Kearns, David T., and Doyle, Denis P. 1988. *Winning the brain race: A bold plan to make our schools competitive.* San Francisco: Institute for Contemporary Studies.

Keller, Evelyn Fox. 1983. *A feeling for the organism: The life and work of Barbara McClintock.* New York: W. H. Freeman.

Ketcham, Ralph. 1987. *Individualism and public life: A modern dilemma.* Oxford: Basil Blackwell.

King, Ynestra. 1983. Toward an ecological feminism and a feminist ecology. In Joan Rothschild (Ed.), *Machina ex dea: Feminist perspectives on technology,* 118–29. New York: Pergamon.

————. 1989. The ecology of feminism and the feminism of ecology. In Judith Plant (Ed.), *Healing the Wounds: The promise of ecofeminism*. Philadelphia and Santa Cruz: New Society Publishers.

Kleinfeld, Judith Smilg. 1979. *Eskimo school on the Andreafsky: A study of effective bicultural education*. New York: Praeger.

Kliebard, Herbert M. 1986. *The struggle for the American curriculum: 1893–1958*. Boston: Routledge and Kegan Paul.

Kropotkin, Peter. 1914/1972. *Mutual aid: A factor in evolution*. London: Penguin.

Kubey, Robert, and Csikszentmihalyi, Mihaly. 1990. *Television and the quality of life: How viewing shapes everyday experience*. Hillsdale: NJ: Lawrence Erlbaum Associates.

Kyle, Regina M. J. 1988. *Innovation in education*. Louisville: Gheens Professional Development Academy.

Lappe, Frances Moore, and Collins, Joseph. 1977. *Food first: Beyond the myth of scarcity*. Boston: Houghton Mifflin.

Lasch, Christopher. 1977. *Haven in a heartless world*. New York: Basic Books.

————. 1989. Progress: The last superstition. *Tikkun* (May/June).

Leacock, Eleanor. 1969. *Teaching and learning in city schools*. New York: Basic Books.

Leestma, Robert. 1987. *Japanese education today: A report of the U.S. study of education in Japan*. Washington, D.C.: U.S. Department of Education.

Levin, Henry, and Rumberger, Russell. 1983. The low-skill future of high tech. *Technology Review* (August/September):18–21.

Levine, Arthur. 1981. *When dreams and heroes died*. San Francisco: Jossey-Bass.

Lipsitz, Joan. 1984. *Successful schools for young adolescents*. New Brunswick, NJ: Transaction Books.

Lovelock, J. E. 1979. *Gaia: A new look at life on earth*. Oxford: Oxford University Press.

McDermott, R. P. 1974. Achieving school failure: An anthropological approach to illiteracy and social stratification. In George Spindler (Ed.), *Education and cultural process: Toward an anthropology of education*,82–118. New York: Holt, Rinehart, and Winston.

McDermott, Raymond P., and Gospodinoff, Kenneth. 1979. Social contexts for ethnic borders and school failure. In A. Wolfgang (Ed.), *Nonverbal behavior*. New York: Academic Press.

McDill, Edward L.; Natriello, Gary; and Pallas, Aaron M. 1986. A population at risk: Potential consequences of tougher school standards for student dropouts. *American Journal of Education* 94:135–81.

MacIntyre, Alasdair C. 1981. *After virtue: A study in moral theory.* Notre Dame, IN: University of Notre Dame Press.

McKnight, John L. 1984. John Deere and the bereavement counselor. Fourth Annual E. F. Schumacher Lecture, New Haven, CT.

McNeil, Linda. 1987. School knowledge and the cost of accountability. Presentation given on November 9, 1987 at the University of Wisconsin-Madison.

MacPherson, C. B. 1962. *The political theory of possessive individualism: Hobbes to Locke.* London: Oxford University Press.

Madden, Nancy A.; Slavin, Robert E.; Karweit, Nancy L.; Liverman, Barbara J. 1989. Restructuring the urban elementary school. *Educational Leadership* 46, no. 5 (February):14–20.

Maeroff, Gene. 1988. *An imperiled generation: Saving urban schools.* Princeton, NJ: Carnegie Foundation for the Advancement of Teaching.

Makarenko, Anton. 1976. *His life and his work in education.* Compiled by Valentin Kumarin. Translated from the Russian by Katharine Judelson. Moscow, USSR: Progress Publishers.

Mander, Jerry. 1978. *Four arguments for the elimination of television.* New York: Morrow Quill.

Mann, Horace. 1848. *Twelfth annual report of the board of education.* Boston: Dutton and Wentworth State Printers.

Matute-Bianchi, Maria Eugenia. 1986. Ethnic identities and patterns of school success and failure among Mexican-descent and Japanese-American students in a California high school: An ethnographic analysis. *American Journal of Education* (November):233–55.

Merchant, Carolyn. 1980. *The death of nature: Women, ecology, and the scientific revolution.* San Francisco: Harper and Row.

Metz, Mary H. 1978. *Classrooms and corridors: The crisis of authority in desegregated secondary schools.* Berkeley: University of California Press.

———. 1986. *Different by design: The context and character of three magnet schools.* New York: Routledge and Kegan Paul.

Mewes, Horst. 1985. The Green Party comes of age. *Environment* 27, no. 5:13–39.

Meyer, John. 1977. Education as an institution. *American Journal of Sociology* 83:55–77.

————. 1980. Levels of educational systems and schooling effects. In C. E. Bidwell and D. M. Windham (Eds.), *The analysis of educational productivity: Issues in microanalysis*, 15–63. Cambridge, MA: Ballinger.

Meyer, John, and Rowan, Brian. 1983. The structure of educational organizations. In Victor Baldridge and Terrence Deal (Eds.), *The dynamics of organizational change in education*. Berkeley: McCutchan.

Mollner, Terry. 1988. The third way is here. *In Context* 19:54–59.

Moore, Donald, and Davenport, Susan. 1988. *The new improved sorting machine*. Madison, WI: National Center on Effective Secondary Schools.

Naess, Arne. 1985. Identification as a source of deep ecological attitudes. In Michael Tobias (Ed.), *Deep ecology*, 256–70. San Diego: Avant Press.

National Commission on Excellence. 1983. *A nation at risk: The imperative for educational reform*. Washington, D.C.: U.S. Government Printing Office.

Newmann, Fred M. 1975. *Education for citizen action: Challenge for secondary curriculum*. Berkeley: McCutchan.

Newmann, Fred M., and Oliver, Donald W. 1967. Education and community. *Harvard Educational Review* (Winter):61–106.

Newmann, Fred M., and Rutter, Robert A. 1985a. *A profile of high school community service programs*. Madison, WI: Wisconsin Center for Education Research.

————. 1985b. *The effects of high school community service programs on students' social development*. Madison, WI: Wisconsin Center for Education Research.

Nisbet, Robert. 1973. *The social philosophers: Community and conflict in Western thought*. New York: Thomas Y. Crowell.

Noble, Kenneth B. 1986. Study finds that 60 percent of 11 million who lost jobs got new ones. *New York Times* (February 27, 1986):1, 15.

Noddings, Nel. 1984. *Caring: A feminine approach to ethics and moral education*. Berkeley: University of California Press.

Ogbu, John U. 1978. *Minority education and caste: The American system in cross-cultural perspective*. New York: Academic Press.

Oliver, Donald, and Gershman, Kathleen. 1989. *Education, modernity, and fractured meaning: Toward a theory of process education*. Albany: State University of New York Press.

O'Neill, John. 1990. Piecing together the restructuring puzzle. *Educational Leadership*, 47, no. 7 (April), 4–10.

Ophuls, William. 1977. *Ecology and the politics of scarcity: Prologue to a political theory of the steady state.* San Francisco: W. H. Freeman.

Parent, Elizabeth Ann. 1985. Review of *Between sacred mountains: Stories and lessons from the land. Harvard Educational Review* 55, no. 1 (February):134–37.

Parsons, Talcott. 1959. The school class as a social system: Some of its functions in American society. *Harvard Educational Review* 29, no. 4 (Fall):297–318.

Peshkin, Alan. 1977. *Growing up American: Schooling and the survival of community.* Chicago: University of Chicago Press.

———. 1986. *God's choice: The total world of a fundamentalist Christian school.* Chicago: University of Chicago Press.

Pittsburgh New Futures Board of Directors. 1988. *Pittsburgh New Futures Proposal.* Pittsburgh: Author.

Porritt, Jonathon. 1984. *Seeing green: The politics of ecology explained.* New York: Basil Blackwell.

Portland Investment. 1989. *Moving toward institutional change: Lessons from the experiences of Portland, Oregon.* Portland, Oregon: Author.

Postel, Sandra. 1987. Stabilizing chemical cycles. In Lester R. Brown (Ed.), *State of the world: 1987,* 157–76. New York: Norton.

Potter, David. 1954. *People of plenty.* Chicago: University of Chicago Press.

Purpel, David E. 1989. *The moral and spiritual crisis in education: A curriculum for justice and compassion in education.* Granby, MA: Bergin and Garvey.

Radin, Paul. 1953. *The world of primitive man.* New York: Henry Schuman.

Raizen, Senta A. 1988. *Increasing educational productivity through improving the curriculum.* Rutgers, NJ: Center for Policy Research in Education.

Ratzki, Anne. 1988. The remarkable impact of creating a school community: One model of how it can be done: An interview with Anne Ratzki. *American Educator* (Spring):10–17ff.

Raywid, Mary Anne. 1988. Community and schools: A prolegomenon. *Teachers College Record* 90, no. 2 (Winter):197–210.

Reese, William J. 1986. *Power and the promise of school reform: Grassroots movements during the progressive era.* Boston: Routledge and Kegan Paul.

Reich, Robert B. 1983. *The next American frontier.* New York: New York Times Books.

Riva, Joseph P., Jr. 1983. *World petroleum resources and reserves.* Boulder, CO: Westview Press.

Rock Point Community School. 1984. *Between sacred mountains: Stories and lessons from the land.* Tucson: University of Arizona Press.

Rodriguez, Richard. 1982. *Hunger of memory: The education of Richard Rodriguez.* New York: Bantam.

Rohlen, Thomas P. 1983. *Japan's high schools.* Berkeley: University of California Press.

Rutter, Robert A. 1987. NA-WAY-EE, The Center School. In *Dropout prevention and recovery: Fourteen case studies.* Madison, WI: National Center on Effective Secondary Schools.

Sagan, Eli. 1985. *At the dawn of tyranny: The origins of individualism, political oppression, and the state.* New York: Knopf.

Sahlins, Marshall D. 1965. On the sociology of primitive exchange. In *The relevance of models for social anthropology.* Association of Social Anthropolgists. New York: Praeger.

———. 1972. *Stone-age economics.* Hawthorne, NY: Aldine de Gruyter.

Sale, Kirkpatrick. 1985. *Dwellers in the land: The bioregional vision.* San Francisco: Sierra Club Books.

———. 1987. Ecofeminism: A new perspective. *The Nation* (September 26, 1987):302–05.

———. 1988. Deep ecology and its critics. *The Nation* (May 14, 1988):670–75.

Salleh, Ariel Kay. 1984. Deeper than deep ecology: The eco-feminist connection. *Environmental Ethics* 6, no. 4:339–45.

Samuelson, Robert J. 1988. Perils of the drought. *Newsweek* 112 (September 5, 1988):53.

Sarason, Seymour 1982. *The culture of the school and the problem of change,* 2nd ed. Boston: Allyn and Bacon.

———. 1990. *The predictable failure of educational reform: Can we change course before it's too late?* San Francisco: Jossey-Bass.

Satin, Mark. 1987. Fear and longing at the Green gathering. *New Options* 40 (June 30, 1987):1–4.

Schlechty, Phillip C. 1989. Presentation before New Futures representatives at the Gheens Professional Development Academy, March 23, 1989.

Schlechty, Phillip C.; Ingwerson, Donald W.; and Brooks, Terry I. 1988. Inventing professional development schools. *Educational Leadership* (November):28–31.

Schofield, Janet Ward. 1982. *Black and white in school: Trust, tension, or tolerance?* New York: Praeger.

Schofield, Janet Ward, and Sagar, H. Andrew. 1979. The social context of learning in an interracial school. In Ray R. Rist (Ed.), *Desegregated schools: Appraisals of an American experiment*, 155–99. New York: Academic Press.

Schrag, Francis. 1986. Educational and historical materialism. *Interchange* 17, no. 3 (Autumn):42–52.

Schumacher, E. F. 1973. *Small is beautiful: Economics as if people mattered*. New York: Harper and Row.

Schwartz, Frances. 1981. Supporting or subverting learning: Peer group patterns in four tracked schools. *Anthropology and Education Quarterly* 12, no. 2:99–121.

Seabury, Jane. 1987a. Typical families' income has fallen. *Washington Post*, November 29, 1987.

———. 1987b. Middle class dream fades for some. *Washington Post*, January 4, 1987.

Sedlak, Michael W; Wheeler, Christopher W.; Pullin, Diana C.; Cusick, Philip A. 1986. *Selling students short: Classroom bargains and academic reform in the American high school*. New York: Teachers College Press.

Sennett, Richard, and Cobb, Jonathan. 1972. *The hidden injuries of class*. New York: Knopf.

Shephard, Paul. 1982. *Nature and madness*. San Francisco: Sierra Club Books.

Sizer, Theodore. 1986. Rebuilding: First steps by the Coalition of Essential Schools. *Phi Delta Kappan* (September):38–42.

Smith, Adam. 1947. The wealth of nations. In Saxe Commins and Robert N. Linscott (Editors), *Man and the state: The political philosophers*, 328–407. New York: Washington Square Press.

Smith, Gregory A. 1987a. Madison Memorial School-Within-a-School. In *Dropout prevention and recovery: Fourteen case studies*. Madison, WI: National Center on Effective Secondary Schools.

———. 1987b. Sierra Mountain High School. In *Dropout prevention and recovery: Fourteen case studies*. Madison, WI: National Center on Effective Secondary Schools.

Smith, Huston. 1982. *Beyond the post-modern mind*. New York: Crossroad.

Spindler, George D. 1974. The transmission of culture. In George D. Spindler (Ed.), *Education and cultural process: Toward an anthropology of education*. New York: Holt, Rinehart, and Winston.

Spretnak, Charlene. 1986. *The spirituality of Green politics.* Santa Fe: Bear and Company.

Spring, Joel. 1976. *The sorting machine: National educational policy since 1945.* New York: Longman.

Stack, Carol B. 1975. *All our kin: Strategies for survival in a Black community.* New York: Harper and Row.

Stedman, Lawrence C., and Smith, Marshall S. 1983. Recent reform proposals for American education. *Contemporary Education Review* 2, no. 2 (Fall):85–104.

Steinetz, Victoria Anne, and Solomon, Ellen Rachel. 1986. *Starting out: Class and community in the lives of working-class youth.* Philadelphia: Temple University Press.

Stevenson, Robert. 1987. Schooling and environmental education: Contradictions in purpose and practice. In I.M. Rowbottom (Ed.), *Environmental education: Practice and possibility.* Geelong, Victoria: Deakin University Press.

Stigler, James W., and Stevenson, Harold W. 1991. How Asian teachers polish each lesson to perfection. *American Educator* (Spring):12–20ff.

Task Force on Education for Economic Growth. 1983. *Action for excellence: A comprehensive plan to improve our nation's schools.* Denver: Education Commission of the States.

Timar, Thomas. 1989. The politics of school restructuring. *Phi Delta Kappan* (December):265–75.

Tonnies, Ferdinand. 1955. *Community and association.* London: Routledge and Kegan Paul.

Turkel, Susan B., and Abramson, Theodore. 1986. Peer Tutoring and mentoring as a drop-out prevention strategy. *Clearing House* 60 (October):68–71.

Turnbull, Colin M. 1972. *The mountain people.* New York: Simon and Schuster.

Twentieth Century Fund Task Force on Federal Elementary and Secondary Education Policy. 1983. *Making the grade.* New York: The Twentieth Century Fund.

U.S. Department of Commerce. 1988. *Statistical abstracts of the United States.* Washington D.C.

U.S. Department of Energy. 1988. *International energy annual.* Washington, D.C.

U.S. News and World Report. 1988. America's hidden poor. (January 11, 1988):18–24.

Vidich, Arthur J., and Bensman, Joseph. 1968. *Small town in mass society: Class, power, and religion in a rural community.* Princeton, NJ: Princeton University Press.

Wachtel, Paul L. 1988. *The poverty of affluence: A psychological portrait of the American way of life.* Philadelphia: New Society Publishers.

Waller, Willard. 1932/1967. *The sociology of teaching.* New York: John Wiley and Sons.

Wax, Murray L.; Wax, Rosalie H.; and Dumont, Robert V. 1964. Formal education in an American Indian community. Supplement to *Social Problems* 11:4.

Wehlage, Gary G. 1987. The Media Academy. In *Dropout prevention and recovery: Fourteen case studies.* Madison, WI: National Center on Effective Secondary Schools.

Wehlage, Gary G.; Rutter, Robert A.; Smith, Gregory A.; Lesko, Nancy; Fernandez, Ricardo R. 1989. *Reducing the risk: Schools as communities of support.* New York: Falmer.

Weis, Lois. 1985. *Between two worlds: Black students in an urban community college.* Boston: Routledge and Kegan Paul.

————. 1988. The 1980s: Deindustrialization and change in white working class male and female youth culture forms. *Metropolitan Education* 5 (Fall):82–117.

Wigginton, Eliot. 1985. *Sometimes a shining moment: The Foxfire experience.* New York: Anchor.

Wilcox, Kathleen. 1982. Differential socialization in the classroom: Implications for equal opportunity. In George Spindler (Ed.), *Doing the ethnography of schooling,* 456–88. New York: Holt, Rinehart, and Winston.

William T. Grant Foundation. 1988. *The forgotten half: Non-college youth in America.* Washington, D.C.

Williams, Raymond. 1961. *The long revolution: An analysis of democratic, industrial, and cultural changes transforming our society.* New York: Columbia University Press.

Williams, William Appleman. 1980. *Empire as a way of life: An essay on the causes and character of America's present predicament along with a few thoughts about an alternative.* New York: Oxford University Press.

Willis, Paul. 1977. *Learning to labor: How working class kids get working class jobs.* New York: Columbia University Press.

Index